LIKE A CAT WITH NINE LIVES
(The Near-Death Experiences Of A Career Cop)

A NOVEL BY
Sergeant Howard A. Monta, Seattle P.D.
(Ret.)
With Liz Monta

AmErica House
Baltimore

First printing

ISBN: 1-58851-575-3
PUBLISHED BY AMERICA HOUSE BOOK PUBLISHERS
www.publishamerica.com
Baltimore

Printed in the United States of America

This book is dedicated to the memory of
Seattle Police Officer Jerry Wyant

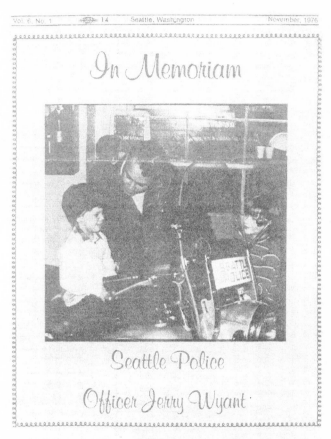

Vol. 8, No. 1   14   Seattle, Washington   November, 1976

In Memoriam

Seattle Police
Officer Jerry Wyant

This, the November 1976 edition of the **Guardian** is dedicated to the memory of Seattle Police Officer Jerry Wyant who gave his life in the line of duty on October 26th. (The above photograph of Jerry was taken at a RAG Christmas Party. The children are unidentified.)

The above Memoriam was published in the November 1976 issue of *The Guardian* — a publication of the Seattle Police Officers' Guild. It is reproduced with the permission of *The Guardian*. Officer Wyant's fatal motorcycle accident is described in Chapter Eight of this book.

CONTENTS

FOREWORD

The reader who overlooks this Foreword might mistakenly interpret *Like A Cat With Nine Lives* to be a fiction novel. Be advised that the adventure stories of the central character, Howard, are factual; and the entire novel is based upon his life experiences. The names of some characters have been changed for issues of privacy.

This book provides a privileged look into the maturing process and the law enforcement career of a not-so-ordinary police officer. It will be of interest to any person who harbors curiosity about the following: the make-up (fabric) of cops; what attracts them to their profession; how they cope with the danger; how they deal with the disappointment; how they catch criminals; how they survive; and why these dedicated individuals remain in the profession. Most importantly, evidence will be provided to the reader that no matter how bold and adventurous a police officer is in the performance of his or her duties, pure fate oftentimes dictates whether the officer survives or dies. Some live through the most serious life-threatening experiences, while the lives of others slip away during relatively low-risk events. Things unfold as if there were a predetermined master plan. Call it fate, or call it the mighty hand of a higher power—whichever makes you comfortable.

Chapter by chapter, *Like A Cat With Nine Lives* will answer most of the questions for those who wish to know *what makes cops tick*. From Chapter One, "A Daredevil Growing Up," through Chapter Twelve, "The End," the reader is given a very personal insight relating to where cops come from, and how the lives of men and women in law enforcement are defined by their profession.

CHAPTER 1

A Daredevil Growing Up

It wasn't easy being an awkward and chubby little fourth and fifth grader in the mid-1940s. In addition to his unfortunate physical appearance, the chubby kid was self-conscious about being saddled with the first name of "Howard." It wasn't that he thought his name was so bad, it was just that all of the popular kids had names like Joey, Larry, Mike, John, Tony, and Jimmy. He was the only kid he knew of named Howard. Being poor, despite having a hard-working father, didn't help matters; but that was the easy part. These circumstances caused an obsession to strive for acceptance that seldom occurred. He turned most of his energy toward excelling in his schoolwork—a blessing in disguise.

Adding to the devastating humiliation was the unintentional cruelty of the other children. Kids of that age have not had the opportunity to develop the human trait known as compassion. Compassion cannot be taught—it evolves from personally experiencing the harm and disappointment that enables humans to place themselves in the shoes of someone who is suffering. There are freaks of society who never acquire compassion for others. These deviates are the murderers, rapists, robbers, and thieves—just to name a few. Howard's home was less than a block from his school. There was a constant worry about the other kids seeing his mother; because on one occasion, a brat blurted out, "Look—Fatso Howie's mom is fat too."

Life at home was good, considering the lack of worldly possessions and the fact that both parents came from extremely poor backgrounds. Howard's father was born and raised in a tent on the Coeur d'Alene Indian Reservation in Idaho in the early 1900s. His mother was from a German family of ten children in Milwaukee. Howard's parents treated him as if he were something special, probably because he entered this world very late in his mother's childbearing years.

Upon graduating to junior high school, Howard had been transformed from the short, chubby kid to a 5-foot-8-inch "string bean" of 125 pounds. Cleveland Jr. High School was a part of the same facility as the high school, and the 1950s was the decade of the bullies. It was vitally important to establish a pecking order, either by bluff or through physical challenges. The *Charles Atlas* magazine advertisements were very meaningful, as Howard could relate to the "90-pound weakling" who was pictured as having sand kicked in his face by the beach bully. To make the ads more hurtful, the bully always walked away with the beautiful girl in the sexy bathing suit. The ads promised that the weakling could reverse that role, and kick that bully's butt, by following the *Charles Atlas* weightlifting routine.

When he was thirteen, Howard talked his father into buying a 110-pound barbell set, and bodybuilding became an obsession. Progress was slow, but steady. Episodes of bullying rapidly declined until coming to a complete halt. By the time the formerly pudgy kid reached his sophomore year, he was bench pressing 225 pounds, and dead lifting 375 pounds, at a body weight of 175 pounds. The meanest kids in school chose not to jeopardize their reputations by testing this mean-looking machine. When this kid with his "Princeton" hair style (flat on top with sides combed in a "duck tail") wore his T-shirt, and blue jeans pulled down below the crack of his butt, nobody wanted to test him as he strutted and flexed around the school. This was the nostalgic image from which the Fonz (Henry Winkler), of the television show *Happy Days*, patterned his character.

This newfound confidence was a profound change from the awkward and unpopular grade-school kid. The new Howard was an adventurous risk taker, but he still maintained that deep-rooted need to impress and please others. He supported a three-tone 1955 Dodge V8 by working for his father on weekends, and for a blueprint company after school. That yellow, black and white Dodge was lowered, had skirts on the rear fenders, and dual pipes with the mufflers removed. Speeding was a thrill. One hundred ten miles per hour became a regular routine, especially on the straight and flat Lake Washington Floating Bridge. A new and exciting venture was experimenting with alcoholic beverages—a seemingly harmless indulgence that soon became a necessary part of his social activity.

In his senior year, Howard earned the respect of the toughest kids in school; but that wasn't enough. He had his eye on Flower, a fifteen-year-old freshman. Flower possessed all of the criteria necessary for goddess status in the 1950s. "Thin" was definitely not "in" during this era when Marilyn Monroe and Jayne Mansfield were idolized. For a girl to be oversized in a particular body area was not a detriment, and Flower's appearance could best be described as "voluptuous." It was an image builder for Howard to drive Flower around while she wore her tightest of cashmere sweaters. The other guys must have been green with envy. When he would ask her if she would go to the drive-in movie on the weekend, the coolest of all of the "makeout" spots, she would always ask, "Did you get the case of beer yet?"

"I'll get some beer somehow," he would reply. Purchasing beer was a challenge. One method that worked most of the time was to give a drunk some money for wine in return for buying the beer. Sometimes the drunk would just disappear with all of the money. Disappointment was a routine emotion for a kid with rapidly developing biological urges, as Flower would never drink enough beer to get careless. Howard was permitted to touch the coveted trophies, but he was never allowed to fulfill his wildest dreams.

Howard had an intense dislike for cops, partly due to the many speeding tickets he accrued, but mainly because cops seemed to have more free time in the 50s to check up on the wild teenagers. One example was when he and his best friend, Dennis, were on a double date. The only booze they were able to procure was a pint bottle of cheap whiskey. The teens were approaching a drive-in movie when two reserve deputy sheriffs pulled the Dodge over. The first question they asked was, "You kids got any booze?"

The standard answer was, "No, sir!"

"Ok, everyone out of the car." As the deputies searched the interior of his Dodge, Howard thought that he was about to be busted. His parents, as well as the parents of Dennis and the girls, would have to come and pick them up. To his astonishment, the deputies finished their search and said, "Ok, you kids can go, but don't let us catch you out after curfew."

Back in the car, and breathing a sigh of relief, Howard asked, "Where in the hell did you hide that bottle?" With an ear-to-ear grin on his face, Dennis reached into his flight boot (he worked at a flying service after school) and pulled the bottle out. After that, Howard never again complained about Dennis not wearing more stylish footwear. This was one of too many contacts with the cops. If anyone had suggested that he would someday be a cop, he would have laughed, or become angry. His dislike for the police was so intense he would have walked around the block just to avoid passing by anyone with a uniform and badge.

At the time, this mischievous kid did not realize that the experience of evolving from the picked-on fat kid to a strong and confident teenager had conditioned him to crave excitement. He thrived on taking risks and stretching limits. In his desperation to place himself "on the edge," Howard would swim out of the guarded area of beach parks, to the middle of the lakes. He would climb in unsafe areas and operate his car with reckless abandon. Another result of having been the object of teasing and physical cruelty was a lifelong resentment of anyone who would victimize a vulnerable person.

A few years later, as a law enforcement officer, Howard was to learn just how cowardly the bullies in society were, when faced with even odds. He experienced a preview of such cowardice when he realized that the school bullies would seek easier prey once Howard had taken on a muscular and confident appearance. As a police officer, the role he would never have believed he would fill, Howard would later grow to know just how meek the most brutal of criminals became when he confronted them. Another thing Howard did not realize until later in life was that his propensity for taking risks would lead to innumerable dangerous experiences and nine incidents wherein death would be more likely than survival.

After graduation, the seventeen-year-old couldn't convince his parents that he was all grown up. To achieve independence, he joined the U.S. Air Force. This decision led to two of the many near-death experiences Howard would face.

Howard as a thirteen-year-old 'skinny string bean' with pet crow — before starting his weightlifting routine.

CHAPTER 2

The Military Experience

It did not take long for the wild Seattle boy to realize that the military was not a piece of cake. He and the other recruits were transported by bus to Parks Air Force Base. Howard didn't know exactly where the base was located. He thought it was somewhere in California, near Oakland. The T.I. *(Training Instructor)* met the group of "boots" at the Greyhound Bus Depot. He was a lean and muscular little man in his twenties. His uniform was impeccable, and the reflection of the sun was near blinding in the spit-shine on his jump-boots. This man's face was so hard that it looked as if it had been carved from stone with a dull chisel. Howard thought it would be polite to introduce himself and shake hands. That approach didn't work. The T.I. *(Training Instructor)* drew his hand back and said, "If that is gum in your mouth, spit it out now, you idiot!"

Howard responded, "OK," and spat his gum to the ground.

"What did you say? When you address me, it is YES, SIR!"

The shocked teenager responded, "OK."

"WHAT?" the disturbed T.I. bellowed!

"I mean YES, SIR!"

"That's better," he sneered. "Did the rest of you mamas' boys learn anything?"

The group shouted in unison, "YES, SIR!" That was a tough way to start a relationship with the instructor, and it formed the basis for this young man's negative feelings about military discipline for the remainder of his life. *This is BULLSHIT!* he thought. Not only did Howard have to give up his social drinking, his hot Dodge V8, and Flower—he had to deal with this T.I. for a full four weeks of boot camp.

It was a motley looking crew that arrived with Howard that day. They were dressed in all styles, from "real cool threads" to down-on-the-farm grubbies. There were manners of speech that were difficult for the West Coast native to understand. They made a stab at marching in step to their barracks, while the T.I. laughed, swore, and mimicked them. After introduction to their crowded bunkroom, the T.I. forewarned the group about the standard four-week routine. He explained how they would be up by 5 a.m. *(or earlier)*, scrub the barracks, march and exercise, and pick up pebbles on the base grounds when there was nothing constructive to do. This picture is identical to what most young people of that era had seen in the movies. Howard's problem was that he had only seen cowboy and comedy movies as a little kid; and since becoming a teen, he had only attended drive-in movies, where he paid little attention to the screen. "Come on, you bunch of greasy looking scum," the T.I. said as he herded the group from their barracks to the base barbershop. The sheep were seated and sheared clean in groups of six. As if Howard's ego had not suffered enough already, now his long sideburns and "duck's ass" locks were lying on the floor. There was not a trace of pride and confidence left in him. He did not realize it, but that was exactly what introduction to boot camp was supposed to do. Four insane weeks, and then it was off to technical school in Wichita Falls, Texas, to learn the business of towing targets.

Tests had determined that his weakest skill level was in the mechanical fields, so it should have been no surprise to Howard that he was assigned to a career field that involved mechanical work on airplanes. His job in the Air Force would consist of general maintenance on the B-26 Bomber—one of the fastest of reciprocating engine planes that was used toward the end of World War II, and in the Korean War. Compared to the new jet-engine bomber *(B-47)* Howard had observed at Boeing

Airplane Company from his family home on Beacon Hill, the B-26 looked pretty ancient. Howard was to be trained as a crewmember who launched and released targets for air-to-air and ground-to-air gunnery. This was facilitated through the use of two hydraulic cable reels located in the rear gunner's compartment—behind the bomb compartment. The bomb bay was used to store the banner targets for air-to-air practice and sleeve targets for ground-to-air practice. The gunner's compartment was a cramped space, containing radio equipment, a few targets, release sleeves, and other tools. With the World War II parachute strapped on his back, all movements involved in the process of launching targets were a challenge.

Howard had performed competently with the military carbine during boot camp as a result of many Red Ryder B-B-Gun battles fought while he was growing up. Because of his crewmember status, Howard was assigned an old Army 45-caliber semi-automatic pistol; but first he had to be trained to use it. The sight of that gun, let alone the thunderous explosion and mule-like recoil, was enough to cause second thoughts about pulling the trigger. After pitifully sketchy classroom firearms training, an ancient master sergeant took the new kids to the gun range. This burly sergeant was the picture of masculinity, with his sleeve full of stripes, rugged square jaw, and the weathered face of an angry brute. This man could have been the future inspiration for the "Tasmanian Devil" cartoon character. Unlike the T.I. at basic training, the firearms instructor was not a "spit and polish" military specimen. He was overweight, with an unpressed and partially untucked shirt, and a protruding beer belly. The nasty old guy pounded an ammunition clip into the pistol and in a thick, gravely voice said, "Here kid, let's see you blast that target [a small bull's-eye target 25 yards away]." Howard took a strong stance, with feet spread and arms outstretched—mimicking what he had observed in the training movie; but inside, he was terrified. The sergeant finally yelled, "What the hell are you waiting for? Empty that fucking gun!"

The shaky recruit closed his eyes and jerked the trigger back, setting off a colossal explosion. It was every bit as horrifying as he had anticipated—like having the neighborhood bully land a good punch on his upper chest area. *I can do this!* he thought, and he squeezed off the remainder of rounds in the clip.

"Where in the hell are the holes in the target?" the sergeant bellowed. "You are supposed to hit the goddamn thing. Give me that fuckin' gun!" He grabbed the pistol from Howard's hand and pounded another ammunition clip into the handgrip. Taking a majestic shooter's stance *(right arm outstretched and left arm resting artistically on his hip)*, he fired off nine rounds in rapid succession. To everyone's amazement, the harsh recoil did not affect the sergeant. The recruits stood with mouths open at such a display of brute strength and skill—until it became apparent that only two bullets had struck the outer edge of the target. "Something's wrong with this piece-of-shit weapon—You guys quit standing around and keep practicing!" the sergeant bellowed. Every new kid was too scared of this maniac to even breathe a smile. Howard never was able to hit a target with the Army 45, but the Air Force issued him the weapon and his flight fatigues anyway.

Howard's first duty assignment was the 6th Tow Target Squadron, at Johnson Air Base in Japan *(about 20 miles from Tokyo)*. Though filled with anticipatory excitement, he first had to suffer seventeen days on the aircraft carrier Corregidor—a retired carrier that was being used to transport 325 airmen and a flight deck full of Saber jets to Tokyo. Bunks were stacked three to four high in the dingy living compartments, which were filled with the stench of vomit for the first week. *Isn't the Air Force wonderful?* he thought. What kept him going was the thought of the Japanese girls who would be waiting for their arrival. Rumors of good times were rampant. He would finally experience a real sex act. Those in charge were anticipating the ambitions of the airmen. A systematic plan to put a damper on the fun was activated. The airmen were forced to watch sickening old movies of guys with "elephantiasis", carrying their swollen testicles around in a wheelbarrow, and others with their body parts rotting away from syphilis. They were told that all of these disastrous things would happen to anyone having sex while in Japan. All of the "gruesome-accident" movies the Juvenile

Court Judge forced Howard to watch had not slowed his driving; and all of the shocking "venereal-disease" movies and lectures would not deter him from becoming a "real" man.

The three-day base restriction that was required for processing and indoctrination *(more nasty movies)* had not yet expired when Howard overheard others planning to sneak off base to party. The prospect was too tempting to pass up. The urge to start spending that $65-per-month flight-crew pay, and his $80-to-$90 base pay, was overwhelming. He put on his only set of civilian clothes, making sure to have his assignment orders with him, and went over the fence with a friend. The bars in the town near the base were designed to attract American GIs. The bartenders and bar girls spoke a strange form of broken English. Realizing that Howard was a green rookie, a bar girl (Yoshiko) quickly told him the menu prices, "Cocktail one-hundred yen—short-time 300 yen" (84 cents U.S.).

"What is a short-time?" he asked.

The sweet girl put her hand over her mouth and giggled, "You are cherry boy—Short-time mean you go to bed for short time." She was immediately intrigued with this naïve American and knew that she had to have the kid. It was long after the midnight curfew when the young foreigner found himself in a strange one-room house with no chairs—just pillows and a bed that looked like a plush sleeping bag. Not only was he confused by this culture so different from his homeland, the military jeeps rumbling by made him certain that the MPs would be busting the door down at any moment. "Where is the toilet?"

"What is toilet?" Yoshiko asked.

"You know, I have to piss."

"Oh, Benjo!" she said. "That over there in closet." Howard pushed the closet curtains open and found no toilet—only a hole in the floor.

He complained, "There is no benjo in here."

Yoshiko giggled once again and said, "It right there," pointing to a small hole in the floor. There was no way that Howard would be able to hit that hole while standing up. Humiliated, he sank to his knees and didn't make too big a mess in the closet. A vivid description of the lovemaking that occurred that night would be of no value in a romance novel. The clumsy *(to put it kindly)* act did not exceed one minute in duration. It was embarrassing. All he remembered was a lot of fumbling and grasping, and "Ooh, aah."

"What happen?" Toshiko asked.

"I'm sorry," was the reply.

"You no more cherry boy!"

The world's oldest profession had been an honored one in Japan for centuries. Being an eighteen-year-old in Japan was as exciting as a trip to the candy store for a six-year-old kid. One would be skeptical, perhaps, about a future law enforcement officer being involved with patronizing a prostitute. Howard was able to justify his indiscretions while in the Far East as an attempt to adjust to the culture of the country. Prostitution was an honorable profession, and Howard was trying to do what he thought was the honorable thing. *(When in Rome, do as the Romans do.)*

Before Howard was to leave Japan, he would be given another sign (from somewhere) that trouble would follow him throughout his life, when suddenly the century-old profession of prostitution was ruled illegal. The entire country at first seemed to act in disbelief, then quickly returned to business as usual. Nothing really changed, except the girls would giggle about having to be sneaky. In the year 2000, as the new millennium dawned, Howard would look back upon his law enforcement experience and realize that the world's oldest profession had flourished in the United States much the same way as it had flourished in Japan. The judicial systems in both countries had always made half-hearted attempts to control the unlawful practice, and they had always failed miserably.

The brief tryst with Yoshiko was an enlightening episode *(well worth the 84 cents)*. It did not place Howard in the category of one of the world's greatest lovers, but a kid had to start somewhere. His next challenge was to talk his way back onto the base after curfew, without a pass. He tried to convince the gate guard that he was a new arrival to the base *(while dressed in his civilian clothes)*. This prompted suspicious and angry responses. Military police arrived and transported Howard to his squadron duty officer. His assignment orders were confiscated, and it was base restriction for a week for the rookie.

Howard had to get down to the task of towing targets, anyway. The Sixth Tow Target Squadron was busy towing for the army anti-aircraft gunnery. The sleeve targets resembled a giant sock, towed at seventeen hundred feet behind the aircraft for fifty-caliber and forty-millimeter guns. Sleeves were towed at fifty-one hundred feet for the 120-millimeter cannons. The reason for towing the targets nearly one mile behind the aircraft for the big guns was that if the 120-millimeter shell burst within a block or two of the aircraft, it would likely cause damage or destruction. Banner targets were towed at twenty-one hundred feet for jet fighters firing color-coated rounds, which left stains that were distinctive for each aircraft. Targets were later released over the airfields so that the pilots could be credited for their skill.

Target planes from Japan were sent to Okinawa and Korea for two to three weeks of duty. Howard was given the Korea assignment with only a few months of towing experience. Their three airplanes were based at Kempo Airbase (near the city of Seoul), but the airmen were housed on an adjacent U.S. Army compound that also housed Republic of Korea (ROK) soldiers. The Americans were treated like royalty, because they were perceived to be there primarily to provide a target service for the ROK soldiers. A jeep, along with a Korean Army driver, was assigned especially for their personal use. The day after they arrived, the driver was excitedly loading as many airmen as he could load in his jeep, yelling, "Entertainment! Entertainment!"

Howard jumped in and they raced out of the compound gate. The Jeep seemed to be leaving the populated area, heading toward a rural setting. They arrived at a six-foot wall that surrounded a collection of small, adobe-like buildings, most of which sported flattened American beer cans for roofs. The driver pulled up to the gate and honked wildly. The gate opened, and they parked inside. *This is weird*, thought Howard.

"Bar! Drinking!" shouted the driver as he ushered them to a small dilapidated shack. There were a few scattered tables and a short bar that sported three stools. Howard was able to order an Asahi (Japanese) beer.

The bartender, a middle-aged, short, stocky woman, said, "Girls coming soon."

She was right. Almost immediately, a petite, sweet-looking young thing grabbed him by the arm. Her broken English made her seem even more adorable. "This way," she said as she led him to another ugly building that consisted of a long hallway with several separate rooms. "You have good time with me," she whispered, as she peeled off her clothes. "You hurry." Howard hesitated as he stared at her tiny knobs for breasts. He was confused when she was totally naked. He had no experience with Korean women, but this little shape in front of him, with very little pubic hair, seemed very young.

He asked, "How old are you?" several times, before she reluctantly held up ten fingers, and then a single one, while saying, "Eleben." The eighteen-year-old airman was sickened – he was outraged – he was panicked.

As he exited the room, the young girl asked, "What I do wrong?"

He could only reply, "You are a little girl." Back at the bar he screamed at the driver, "Get me back to the base before I tear this place down! They tried to get me to screw a baby!" The driver recognized that Howard would carry out the threat if he didn't get him out of there right away. Back at the base, he could not find a sympathetic ear. That was the way it was in 1957 Korea, but it was not acceptable to Howard. This experience created a lifelong compassion for the victims of pedophiles and a passionate dislike for anyone who would cause the abuse of a child.

The following day, Howard had not fully recovered from his sad experience in the brothel, when the U.S. soldiers in his barracks attempted to talk him into sneaking under the fence to an off-limits town in back of the compound. They wanted to show him the "the girl of his dreams." They were unusually eager to usher Howard to what appeared to be just another run-down shack with roof shingles made of crushed American beer cans. If he had been more experienced, Howard would have realized that something was up. An old Korean man pulled

Howard to a room that was nearly filled by an American-style bed. "You take off pants and shoes and get in bed," were the instructions. Howard thought, *What have I got to lose?* He waited a few minutes with excited anticipation, wondering what pleasant surprise the army guys had arranged for him.

His heart nearly came to a stop when a woman so ugly that it was impossible to judge her age ran through the door yelling, "I Crazy Mary! I liikeee young American GI." Her arms were outstretched as she ran and jumped on the bed. Crazy Mary's hair looked like the proverbial cartoon of someone who had inserted a finger into an electric socket. Her eyes seemed the size of saucers, and what should have been the white portion of her eyeballs looked like red spider webs. To top off this exotic profile, Mary had no teeth. "You come to me, GI— We makeee beautiful love."

Howard jumped out of bed and grabbed for his pants. He screamed, "Get the hell away from me!"

She grabbed his arm and pleaded, "What wrong GI—you not horny?"

"NO!" he replied as he ran out of the shack with his shoes in his hands. Howard was steamed, because he realized he had been the victim of a cruel joke that was most likely a tradition. The guys were laughing so hard they could barely stay on their feet when Howard arrived at the barracks.

"What's the matter, Howard—didn't you get any?" they teased. The frustration and anger soon subsided, and he joined the rest in the laughter. He had to admit that although he had been the target this time, it was a unique way to break a new guy in—a learning process.

It was not all fun and games. While in Korea, the crew would tow targets for the army of the Republic of South Korea, and they would have to travel the length of South Korea to the end of the Pusan Peninsula to complete their missions. After completing their tow mission, and before flying back to Kempo Field, they would drop a canvas bag of mail to the U.S. Army troops who were working with the ROK soldiers. This was done in a manner similar to launching a target. The only difference was that the pilot would take the aircraft down to within 100 feet of the ocean, fly across a little peninsula, and then, on command, Howard would drop the mailbag onto a parking lot. Most of the time, the mailbag would drop close to the intended area; but sometimes the guys had to climb over fences and stomp through berry bushes to retrieve the mail out of the water.

On this particular occasion they had successfully delivered the mail. Howard felt and heard an explosion, and he observed flame and black smoke billowing from the right engine. The pilot feathered the right propellers. That is a procedure where the engine is shut down and the propellers are turned sideways to reduce air resistance. There was no doubt in the rookie's mind that they were going to crash into the ocean. They were flying so low the whitecaps from the waves appeared to be spraying the aircraft. Howard panicked and deviated from acceptable radio procedure. He keyed his microphone on the command channel and asked the pilot, "Are we going to bail out?"

The displeased pilot answered, "Of course not. We're too low. We are right on the water, but we're ok."

The pilot became more irritated when Howard asked, "Will we land at Pusan?" *(Pusan had an airfield only a few miles away.)* The answer was not what Howard wanted to hear.

The Captain impatiently replied, "Sit back and shut up! We are going to fly back to Kempo, because there are no parts for this old bird at Pusan," he continued. Howard overheard the request to the air command center for an emergency flight plan to Kempo Airfield at an altitude of 6,000 feet. They never came close to reaching that altitude while flying the full length of South Korea. The remaining engine strained and roared as they struggled for altitude a few feet at a time. A direct route was impossible because the bomber had to be maneuvered around hills and mountains. During the flight back to Kempo, Howard was certain that the one good engine would fail and his life would end on a hill in Korea. To Howard's surprise and relief, they landed smoothly with only the left engine operating. He gained a new respect for the ability of the pilots and the power of those R2800 reciprocating engines. This was the first time in his life that Howard believed his death was imminent, but it would not be the last.

Two days later, on his very next mission, the close calls continued. Howard had a target out over a spit of land that extended from the Pusan Peninsula. Forty-millimeter shells were bursting all around the aircraft. He overheard a radio transmission from his pilot to the ground command, "One more burst in front of the aircraft and we are going home."

What am I doing here? Howard thought. What he later learned was that the ROK soldiers were not using radar-controlled sights—they were cranking the guns around by hand and sighting the guns manually. While Howard and the pilot towed for the 120-millimeter guns, the ROKs began blowing up the target on nearly every pass. They were supposed to be shooting for patterns behind the target, but it was more fun to blow it up. This caused a serious workload on the pilot and the hungover kid operating the reels. The procedure for launching the target was for the pilot to slow the aircraft to 110 mph, counting down in increments of five after reaching 125 mph. At 110 mph, the pilot would say, "Launch target—NOW!" and simultaneously raise the tail of the aircraft so that the target would clear the plane as Howard launched the target from a three-foot-square hatch.

The pilot was rushing the launching procedure, and Howard was fumbling while attempting to get the target hooked up and placed into the hatch opening on time. The countdown was at 120 mph, and the end of the sleeve target caught in the wind stream beneath the aircraft. This caused the target to start unraveling out of the tie strings and launch prematurely. While Howard had been frantically trying to pull the target back out of the air stream, the armored cable had wrapped around his hand. As the target launched, the cable ran through his right hand, and it was all he could do to avoid being pulled out of the hatch by the cable. Being towed by a B-26 bomber tied to the end of a runaway cable is one of the least attractive ways to leave this world. He managed to hold on to the side of the hatch door to avoid certain death. The parachute on his back looked like a reject from World War I, but it might open if Howard could remain conscious after being beaten against the side of the bomber. The raw flesh on the palm of his hand was dripping blood. When the pilot felt the concussion of the early launch, he radioed back and asked, "What happened—are you all right?"

Howard answered, "The target slipped out early." He told the pilot, "I'm OK," despite the fact that two fingers were broken and he was in great pain. They should have aborted the mission, but Howard was numb with shock and unable to make a rational decision. The pilot approached him after landing and was stunned when he saw the mutilated hand. Howard was rushed to the base hospital. Near-death experience number two was behind him.

The inactivity that resulted from having a cast on his forearm and hand for a few weeks caused an increase in Howard's consumption of alcoholic beverages. It also provided an opportunity to explore the unforgettably beautiful island of Okinawa. On one of many perfect days in this enchanting paradise, Howard met several of his friends near the boat-moorage area of the local beach. They involved themselves with serious talk and serious drinking. The wages of the airmen were pretty meager. Before they would splurge for the fifty-cent mixed drinks in the bars, the boys would prime themselves on cheap Okinawan Saki. Bottled in used Nippon beer bottles, this strong and contaminated slime was one of many indigenous brews that were declared "off limits" for the U.S. Military. At forty cents per bottle, it was a deal the poorly paid GIs couldn't pass up. The young men became pretty intoxicated. They were nearly ready to go for the cheap bar drinks when they became interested in a sign *(in English)* near one of the boats. It read, **Sightseeing—This boat for charter**. They were just goofy enough to consider including a boat trip in their party plans. A cheap deal was made with the boat owner. The skipper told them, "No drinking on boat!"

"Of course not," they replied with a smirk.

The view of Okinawa from the small boat was more impressive than anyone could have anticipated. The skipper told a story of the "Suicide Cliffs," where women and children leaped to their deaths in fear of the impending invasion by Americans. It was so graphic that it almost sobered the young men. Nonetheless, they continued their consumption of that nasty brew.

They were about one mile offshore when one of his buddies yelled at Howard to quit leaning over the side. Howard was just drunk enough to be outrageously wild. When he got that way, there was nothing he would not do to shock everyone. He immediately screamed and threw himself over the side and into the ocean *(cast on his hand, clothing and all)*. Howard was enjoying the cool ocean water, but the skipper and airmen were alarmed. Before jumping, Howard did not even think about how difficult it would be to return to the boat—or if it would be possible at all. After a momentous physical effort, and excited shouting by his comrades, he was pulled back to the safety of the boat. He convinced the occupants of the boat that he had accidentally fallen overboard. The next day, he had much greater difficulty explaining to a skeptical military doctor why the cast on his hand had melted.

The remainder of Howard's Air Force career was routine, as far as being void of near-death experiences. Routine, that is, if you consider it an everyday occurrence to be thrown into an outdoor, wire holding cage by military police, and subsequently accused of inciting a riot. It seems that the Office of Special Investigation *(OSI)* believed that Howard was one of the instigators of a large-scale fight between Marine and Air Force gentlemen. There were always territorial disputes concerning Okinawan bars and women, but that was not Howard's fault. He finally convinced the investigators that fighting with Marines did not amount to rioting. Later, when Howard would tell friends that in 1957 he fought the "Battle of Okinawa," they would scoff at him and say that the Battle of Okinawa was fought in 1945, during World War II. Howard would explain that in 1957 he fought the U.S. Marines in the bars. "It was a tough fight, but somebody had to fight those marines," he would snicker.

The Far East assignment lasted for twenty months and included temporary duty in Taiwan, Okinawa, Korea, and Southern Japan. The next *(and last)* military assignment was the 2nd Tow Target Squadron at Mitchel Air Force Base, Long Island, New York. It was there that Howard met Liz, the New York girl who would become his wife. The first time he saw her, he knew he could not return to Seattle without her.

Their first meeting was a blind date—a fateful, albeit self-serving, tryst arranged by Liz's friend Ellen. Ellen had become acquainted with Howard and his fellow serviceman and friend Rod a few days earlier. It seemed that Ellen had fallen hard for Rod, but Rod did not own a car, making it difficult for the couple to see each other as often as they would have desired. Howard, however, had a 1953 Oldsmobile that was in mint condition and ran like a bomb. As it turned out, the only way Rod could motivate Howard to be his "wheels" was to get him a date with one of Ellen's friends. Liz had been a reluctant participant in Ellen's little adventure from the outset. She hated blind dates and had never been particularly impressed with Ellen's taste in men. Preparing herself for a distasteful experience, she nevertheless gave in to her friend's pleading and agreed to meet Howard.

The double date was to begin immediately after a ballet class, which Liz and Ellen attended on a weekly basis. The young airmen arrived right on schedule; and after polite introductions, the four teenagers ventured forth into the cool, crisp October evening. The autumn leaves were ablaze in their seasonal colors, and the air was rife with the heady aroma of roasting chestnuts and the anticipatory exhilaration of the approaching holiday season that one can only experience in New York at that time of year. The casual aura of the date belied its significance. The two carefree couples were unaware that they were embarking on a rendezvous with their destinies and beginning a lifelong relationship that only death, in its finality, could end.

Her initial misgivings began to subside, and Liz began to relax as the car wove slowly through traffic along busy Hempstead Turnpike. As they headed to a drive-in restaurant for hamburgers and fries, a carload of young people pulled up in the lane next to Howard's 1953 Oldsmobile Eighty-Eight. The driver raced his engine—the 1950's signal to "go for it." The temptation of such a challenge was too much for the nineteen-year-old kid from Seattle to resist. Howard gunned his engine and took off. After just a few blocks, the other car was falling behind and losing the race. A shocked and angry Liz, sitting beside him in the front seat, shouted, "That cop who just passed by is turning around with his red lights on!"

Howard replied, "He must be after those guys behind us." Howard kept his foot on the accelerator pedal. Noting that the police car had flown by the car he had been racing with, Howard made a fast right turn to a side street, followed by a series of left and right turns. For a while, Howard and his passengers could see the police car two or three blocks away, and parallel to them, as they sped through intersections and red lights. Howard's passengers were screaming at him to stop, but his competitive spirit had risen to an uncontrollable level. Eventually there were no more sightings of the police car, and Howard found his way back to the turnpike.

Continuing leisurely to the restaurant, while stopped for a red traffic signal, they spotted a police officer on the opposite corner. The officer was on foot, animatedly talking on a police call-box telephone. Everyone in the car thought that he was probably receiving an "all points bulletin" relating to the 1953 Oldsmobile that had just eluded the patrol car. The signal turned green. Howard continued straight across the intersection, and no one in the car was surprised when the cop hung the phone up and stepped into the traffic lane—signaling for Howard to stop. What was surprising is that Howard followed the cop's directions and pulled to the curb. He could have continued on his way, because there was no police car in sight for the cop to chase him with. In hindsight, the only explanation for Howard's compliance with the officer's directions at that moment was that a police officer on foot did not challenge his competitive spirit. He rolled down his window as the cop approached. It was evident that this officer of the law was incredulous that the four crazy kids willingly pulled to the curb.

The first words the officer uttered were, "Washington license plates—are you in the military, son?"

"Yes, sir," was the sheepish reply, as Howard handed over his driver's license and military identification card.

Howard was expecting the worst; but the only thing that the cop said after a long hesitation was, "Mitchel Air Force Base, huh? I got a few breaks when I was in the military, so I'll give you one tonight—get out of here and stay out of trouble."

The only thing that Howard could think of saying was,

"Thanks for the break, sir!" The encounter with this cop was the first and only positive contact Howard had experienced with any police officer up to that time. However, the thought of law enforcement as his future profession did not occur to him as even a remote possibility. Liz was put off by his wild antics—especially his driving. It seemed that the more she complained about his risk-taking, the wilder he became. Only because of Ellen's coercion and Howard's persistence did their relationship continue long enough to become serious.

The narrow escape from what could have been serious trouble with the law did not serve to slow the thrill-seeking kid down one bit. His New York girlfriend resisted Howard's determination to win her over; but eventually, against her better judgment, they were married. They moved into military housing on Mitchel Air Force Base, where they enjoyed the camaraderie of other young enlisted couples. Liz later gave birth to their son, Howard III, at the base hospital. Ellen and Rod married a few months after Howard and Liz and had three children. Though the two couples reside at opposite ends of the country, they still maintain their friendship. Howard was discharged from the military and moved to Seattle with his wife and son in early 1960. However, his adventuresome and risk-taking behavior would continue to be an aspect of Howard's personality and an integral part of his life.

Howard's 1953 Oldsmobile 88. The car that he and Liz ran away from the Nassua County, NY Police on their first date.

Howard A. Monta graduating from Air Force Technical School in Wichita Falls, TX, 1956. The commander is unidentified.

Howard A. Monta getting tan in Okinawa in 1958. Note the partial cast on hand from accident while towing targets. Howard was bench pressing 310 pounds during this period.

B-26 Bombers / Tow Target aircraft of the 6th Tow Target Squadron, Johnson Air Force Base, Tokyo, Japan, 1957.

Howard A. Monta at 6th Tow Target Squadron, Johnson Air Force Base, Tokyo, Japan, 1957.

CHAPTER 3

Reserve Deputy and Firefighter

Once separated from the security that the Air Force provided for his family, Howard had to work two jobs until he could find a stable profession. In 1961, a family friend, who happened to be a reserve captain in the King County Sheriff's Department, helped Howard to gain acceptance in a reserve unit that was primarily responsible for juvenile investigations. During that era, the reserve deputy sheriff units were comprised of fourteen to twenty deputies who paid dues. The dues were used to provide and maintain a fully equipped police vehicle. Officers assigned to the juvenile unit paid no dues, because they used the juvenile detective cars, which were normally idle after business hours. The units would staff a two-man patrol car *(no women on street duty in those days)* every night of the week. Reserve deputies had to purchase their own uniforms, leather gear, and gun. They were required to ride at least one uniformed patrol assignment per week.

The first question one would ask about this program is "What would motivate a young man to volunteer time and money to participate in such a program?" The motives varied. Some enjoyed the police authority—and abused it! Others used the police commission and uniform to work lucrative security jobs in taverns and nightclubs. Howard and many others sought the education and experience that was not available to them from any other source. Some had the ultimate goal of landing a full-time job in law enforcement.

There were many thrilling experiences during the three years he served in the King County Sheriff Reserve program, but none as frightening as the night he and his partner had scattered a bunch of kids at a beach keg party on Puget Sound. Howard had separated from his partner, chasing five teens up a heavily wooded, dark, and narrow driveway. Yelling at the scared young men, "Stop or I'll shoot!" was only for effect. As experience would eventually reveal, threats to shoot a running subject usually made them run faster. Shooting at kids running from a kegger would never be a consideration, but Howard was hoping these kids didn't know that. When he was a wild teenager, it was a common belief that cops would shoot you if you tried to run away from a jaywalking ticket.

Howard believed his antique 38-caliber revolver, that he jokingly bragged could shoot around corners because of a bent barrel, was secure in its holster. As he continued running one-half block behind the teens, a deafening explosion rang out that stopped the five fugitives in their tracks. They threw their hands in the air, and one screamed, "We give up officer—You got us—Please don't shoot!" Shocked and puzzled, Howard looked at the pavement and saw his revolver between his feet. The old gun had worked its way out of the secondhand holster and had landed on the firing pin. That caused the accidental discharge, which overwhelmed them all. This gun was manufactured long before the invention of a safety feature that prevents the firing pin from striking the detonator on the bullet until the trigger is pulled. It was a great relief to see all five runners still standing unharmed. Howard's next thoughts were to survey his own body parts for bullet holes.

After realizing there was no physical harm done, embarrassment set in. He felt like digging a hole and crawling into it. The only thing Howard could think of to do next was to yell, "OK, you kids get out of here! And don't ever let me catch you at the beach drinking beer again!"

This was number three of Howard's nine near-death experiences, although at the time Howard considered the mishap a "near-castration" experience. For the gun to land on the firing pin, it would have to hit the ground with the barrel pointing straight up toward his groin area. He realized how lucky he had been.

Howard had been taking civil service exams for the positions of Police Officer and Firefighter in Seattle and Bellevue. He had passed the Bellevue Police written exam and was scheduled for the oral exam when an opportunity for employment with the Seattle Fire Department came up first. Security for his family came before his interest in law enforcement, and so he became a firefighter—but continued his reserve deputy duties for another two years.

Howard's performance as a firefighter was just as aggressive as he would later perform his duties as a cop. That is exactly what the fire department was expecting of its employees in those days. The safety of the firefighters was secondary to ventilating and entering buildings that were fully involved with fire. Once at the fire scene, the orders from the superiors were, "Grab that hose and get in there," no matter how dangerous it looked. During that era, firefighters did not have the advantage of wearing masks and air packs. On the ladder truck to which Howard was assigned, there was a total of three air bottles for use by a minimum of eleven firefighters sent to a house fire. The minimum response was the ladder truck and two engine companies. No one had the opportunity to grab an air pack from the truck, because the rule of the day was, "Get in there and eat that smoke."

In addition to his duties on the ladder truck, Howard sometimes drove the aid car, which responded with the fire trucks. The first aid car he was assigned to was a 1958 Ford station wagon that was later replaced by a panel van. Ironically, he was being paid to drive in a manner that was worse than the driving which caused his appearances in juvenile court. The only rules were to get to an emergency call fast—and he did. On many occasions, when they arrived at a location, the brakes on the station wagon were smoking and inoperative.

On one such emergency run, Howard and his aid car partner, Bud, responded to an industrial fire in the Georgetown area of Seattle. A battalion chief had fallen fifteen feet through the roof of a one-story factory building on to the cement floor. The building occupied one-quarter of a square block, and the fire was enveloping most of the wood-frame construction. When the aid car arrived, Chief Taylor was standing outside. The tough old smoke eater told them, "I'm just fine, but as long as you two are here, we'll use you. Grab that 2½-inch hose and take it inside."

Howard didn't complain, but thought to himself, *Going into that inferno is like entering Satan's parlor. The chief has already fallen through a portion of the collapsing roof, the walls are fully involved, and he wants us to crawl into the middle of it!* The young men followed orders and worked their way to a position near the center of the building. They opened the nozzle and applied a healthy stream of water on the surrounding walls. After ten strenuous minutes of struggling with what felt like wrestling a hundred-foot python, Howard tapped Bud on the shoulder. "I'm out of air—I can't breathe—Let's get out of here."

Bud replied, "You go. I'm ok." He didn't want to leave his partner in that oven, but he was on the verge of passing out. He began crawling for daylight, with his nose a few inches from the floor. The smoke, thick as tapioca pudding, had a pungent, breathtaking odor. Howard would crawl a few yards, stop, choke, and vomit; then crawl a few more yards and dry heave. As he neared an open loading door, he began seeing the rubber boots of other firefighters. He was near exhaustion and still choking, thinking, *Why are these guys not picking me up and getting me out of here?* The reason they were not helping him was that they were too busy making fun of this rookie who couldn't take what they considered "a little smoke."

"You'll get used to it, kid," an old-timer snickered, as he helped Howard to his feet. He was right. During his five-year stint in the SFD, Howard did eat a lot of smoke. What they later learned about the Georgetown industrial fire was that the walls were insulated with a Styrofoam material that was giving off the lung-irritating gas that caused Howard's distress. He suffered sensitivity to all chemical odors from that moment on.

Howard soon experienced another example wherein concern for preservation of property outweighed the concern for the safety of firefighters. He was on the business end of another 2½-inch fire hose, in the middle of a pier and ship fire at Todd's Shipyard on Harbor Island, in Seattle's industrial area. Flames were rising twenty to thirty feet toward the sky from the creosote-coated wood pilings. Howard and his partner were working their way into the heart of the flames. Then he realized they were standing between huge acetylene bottles. These were containers of the gas that fuels acetylene torches for welders. "Acetylene!" he said to his partner. "Come on, let's back out."

As they began to back out of the area, a deputy chief yelled at them, "Get that hose back in there!"

Howard replied, "Those are acetylene bottles and they are getting hot, chief! They are going to blow!"

The chief's compassionate reply was, "Hose them off and get your ass back to that fire."

So much for his concern for my ass, Howard thought.

Between his firefighting experiences and part-time police work, Howard was living the perfect life for one having the disposition of a risk taker; but it wasn't all exhilarating fun and games. Howard's weight dwindled from 215 pounds to 190 pounds during the first three months he was assigned to the aid car. Tragedy after tragedy caused a severe loss of appetite. One of the worst was when the aid car responded to a trailer fire along with the fire trucks. As they arrived, Howard saw a woman in her seventies run out of the burning trailer with her clothes and hair ablaze. While others covered the screaming woman with tarps, Howard grabbed the pump can from the back of the ladder truck and quenched the last of the fire on her clothing. The poor woman was writhing in pain. Her clothes and hair were burned off, her skin blackened and peeled. All of the firefighters were shocked by what they had just witnessed; but as professionals always do, they continued their work extinguishing the trailer fire. Rigorous training and a psychological phenomena called "dissociative response," enables those who are routinely exposed to traumatic events to set their emotions aside while performing stressful work. Dissociation is a defense mechanism that enables one to perform satisfactorily during traumatic experiences.

In an informative report by Daniel Goleman, of the New York Times, published in the Seattle Times, April 17, 1994, Goleman refers to a study by Dr. Charles Marmar, a psychiatrist at the University of California at San Francisco, and Director of the Post-Traumatic Stress Disorder Project at the Veterans Affairs Medical Center in that city. The study of 251 Vietnam veterans suggested a relationship between "dissociative responses during the soldiers' worst combat experiences" and posttraumatic stress disorder. Dissociative response experiences shared by Vietnam veterans participating in the study parallel experiences of firefighters and law enforcement officers. The symptoms described include; "—blanking out during events, time slowing down, events seeming unreal, or feeling as if they were watching themselves from afar or in slow motion."

Now it is known that even though necessary, dissociation has harmful effects. The aforementioned Times report includes comments from Dr. David Spiegel, "a psychiatrist at the Stanford University Medical School and an author of a study of victims of the 1991 Oakland fires." Concerning "dissociation," Spiegel is quoted: "It's a defense that works too well." He says, "People who dissociate are at a greater risk for endangering themselves." The danger Spiegel speaks of is "posttraumatic stress disorder." He recommends that those who are involved in traumatic incidents "—undergo a psychological debriefing afterward." He warns that those who deny a need for debriefing are at greater risk.

Howard had not yet developed the ability to dissociate while performing his distasteful duties; but his wily old veteran partner, Jerry Thompson, was about to teach him the art. His duty to the burn victim did not end at the fire scene. Howard had the responsibility of providing first aid in the back of the aid car during the long ride to the hospital. Remarkably, she remained conscious for the entire trip. There was little he could do except to reassure and comfort her, because the only first aid for burns was the damp cloth covering. That technique for reducing the pain and damage from burns was discovered from studies of World War II Navy burn victims who had to abandon sinking ships. It was discovered that victims who were exposed to the cold ocean water suffered less pain and healed more quickly and thoroughly than those who remained dry in lifeboats.

The scalded, peeling face, with piercing eyes that pleaded for help, would haunt the caring young man for the rest of his life. She repeatedly screamed that she was still on fire. Howard kept his face close to hers and spoke reassurance that she was safe and cared for. The odor of her charred skin combined with the smoky stench from her lungs was overwhelming. Everyone was hoping against hope that she would survive. *(They would learn the next day that she had not.)* Howard felt like crying at the hospital and during the ride back to the station; but what would it look like if a firefighter cried?

Back at the station, they were cleaning up body fluids, charred clothing, and chunks of burned flesh from the back of the aid car. Howard's heart was heavy, and his stomach was wrenching. The rookie thought Jerry was insane when he started joking and trying to make Howard laugh. Jerry made fun of the rookie for getting sick over the incident, and he finally made his point clear when he picked up a large piece of charred flesh and tried to put it down the front of Howard's shirt. A chase ensued out of the garage and through the bunkroom, with Howard yelling, "Get the hell away from me—Are you crazy or what?"

Jerry stopped and began laughing hysterically at his terrified prey, saying, "You have got to loosen up, man, or you ain't going to make it!" Howard finally got the picture. Howard understood Jerry's good intent, and he joined in laughing at himself. Jerry said, "That's better." The veteran firefighter explained that you have to be able to "make light" of tragedy in order to survive. In other words, one must put duty above emotion. From that time on, the rookie was able to do just that. He never was surprised when he heard stories about how "cold and uncaring" some hospital emergency workers seem to be. They become that way so that they can survive another work shift. However, that does not mean that disturbing experiences will not cause psychological harm. As mentioned previously, Dr. Spiegel associates dissociative reactions with posttraumatic stress disorder.

Adjusting well to his new profession, Howard became a proficient and well-liked firefighter. An entire volume could be written, or a television series produced, describing this career that spanned only five years. The camaraderie among the dozen men assigned to his shift was heartwarming, but sometimes embarrassing. With time on their hands between their station duties and emergency calls, teasing and pranks were prevalent.

For example: Dale Smith was greeted by his wife one morning after a 14-hour nightshift—one hand was in his jacket pocket, and he could feel something out of the ordinary. As his wife approached with arms outstretched, Dale pulled a pair of silk panties from his coat pocket, saying, "What's this?"

His wife angrily responded, "Whose are those?"

He sheepishly replied, "I don't know! Are they yours?" He thought for a moment and realized his buddies at the station had zapped him. His wife was not convinced. When Dale complained of his humiliating experience, Howard laughed louder than everyone. This was too funny for words. On his next day off, Howard was going to treat his wife to a chocolate sundae at his favorite old high school delicatessen, the Eagles Roost. He brought two beautiful sundaes to the car. His wife opened the glove box to set her ice cream on the door. A twisted frown appeared on her face. Liz reached into the glove compartment and pulled out that same pair of panties that Dale had displayed at the station. "Who in the hell do these belong to?"

Howard could only respond, "Those dirty bastards at the station!"

"Yeah—Right!" she sneered.

"No! I mean it—They did this to me for a dirty joke," and he went on to tell her of Dale's misfortune. His explanation was reluctantly accepted. Everyone at the fire station was delighted to hear Howard's whining; but Howard took it in stride because he accepted the fact that the new guys take the worst beating.

One thing firefighters are known for is their lifesaving efforts while working at fire scenes, and Howard was looking for his opportunity to be a hero. He was afforded only one chance at a fire rescue during his five-year stint in the fire department. He responded to a hot and smoky apartment fire on the ladder truck. Upon their arrival, a woman was standing in the parking lot, screaming repeatedly, "My baby is in there!" Without hesitation, the brave young firefighter bolted from the side of the truck before it was completely stopped. He rushed into the heat and thick smoke. Not more than ten feet inside the door, Howard had to drop to the floor and crawl to enable him to see and breathe. After checking the couch and chairs in the living room, he crawled into the bedroom.

To his surprise, there was no baby crib. Almost blinded by the smoke, Howard ran his hand over the bed covers on the double bed. He opened the closet door, with still no luck. Beginning to panic, a thought flashed through his mind that the baby could have crawled under the bed, and then succumbed to the suffocating smoke. Hurriedly dropping to his belly, Howard began to feel the floor, as far back under the bed as he could reach. *At last!* he thought, as he grasped a soft little body. Pain shot through his hand and up his arm. He pulled the little body from under the bed. It was not a baby; it was a mean, little French Poodle, and it was trying to bite his hand again.

When the chagrined firefighter exited the apartment with the miniature poodle, the woman cried out, "My Baby! You saved my Baby!" Once again, Howard was set up for more teasing from his associates.

Howard resigned his reserve deputy sheriff commission after three years. He didn't realize it, but his firefighting career was also winding down. He was in his fifth and last year in the Seattle Fire Department when there was a full response to a house in Rainier Valley that was engulfed in flames. Before applying water to the inside of the house, the roof had to be vented so that the heat and smoke would go up and out. Assignment to the ladder truck made that task Howard's responsibility. The old, wood-frame house was constructed on a steep bank, about two stories high on the street side, and four stories high on the backside. Howard noticed that the yard was messy. There were old bicycles, broken chairs, yard tools, large rocks, and miscellaneous junk scattered around the perimeter of the house. There was also a nasty-looking picket fence that attached to both ends of the house in front. They propped the 25-foot ladder on the street side. Howard strapped on his axe and flew up the ladder to the roof.

He chopped away with a vengeance at the old wood shingles. Suddenly, flames leaped up the wood siding; and then the entire roof became engulfed with a dense black smoke. The feeling was like having the wind knocked out of him by a punch in the stomach, and there was no air to breathe when he tried to catch his breath. He became disoriented, unable to determine which side of the house was which, and he couldn't see the ladder. His axe dropped and slid off the roof, and he screamed, "I can't breathe—somebody help me!" The flames were now shooting above the roof.

Howard heard a yell from one of his comrades below, "JUMP!" He thought that the firefighter on the ground did not realize that Howard was seeing his life flash before his eyes and was making fun of his calls for help.

Remembering the picket fence and all of the debris, and knowing that one side *(he didn't know which)* was four stories high, Howard replied, "Fuck you!" to the firefighter who yelled at him. There was no way he was going to jump.

Howard had resolved that his life was about to end. He was barely conscious—about to fall to the roof, when he heard Firefighter Dick Heuer's voice, "Howard—over here!" Howard crawled toward the sound of Dick's voice and found him at the top of the ladder. He was too weak and groggy to negotiate the ladder on his own. Dick had to literally support Howard's weight the entire way down. Howard showed his appreciation to Dick by ungratefully vomiting all over him.

This was his fourth near-death experience; however, it was the first and only incident wherein he had to make the decision to give up his life. He never questioned his decision to die rather than jump into an unknown hazard.

The danger of the job is not what motivated Howard to leave fire fighting. It was the opportunity to attend the University of Washington on a newly offered G.I Bill. He arranged a deal with the Chief to return to the SFD at his option after trying the college routine, and he had not the slightest notion that a law enforcement profession was on the horizon.

CHAPTER 4

College Student and Rookie Cop

Attending the University of Washington in the mid-60s was an eye opener for a 28-year-old ex-airman, ex-firefighter, and ex-reserve cop. Howard decided to let his beard grow so that he would fit in a little bit with the hippie kids with long hair, headbands, and funny-colored sunglasses. Although life was a good deal less exciting, going to school full time and working part time left no time for boredom.

No one was more surprised than Howard when he focused his attention on subjects such as Psychology 101; Sociology 101; Race Relations; Anthropology 101; Calculus; Physics 101; and Chemistry 101. Even more surprising was his appreciation for Shakespeare. He had undergone a transformation from a narrow-minded and self-centered egotist, to a compassionate reformer who thought he could save the law enforcement profession and the rest of the world.

After two years of slavery to the books, financial concerns caused Howard to consider the offer he had been given to return to the Seattle Fire Department. In 1968, he noticed newspaper ads for Seattle Police Department applicants. The temptation was too great. He took the written test in late August and the physical test shortly thereafter. The physical was a breeze; because not only was he bench pressing three hundred pounds, and doing pull-ups with forty-five pounds tied to his waist, he also was running two miles every other day. With his maturity and experience, the SPD jumped at hiring him. One matter that caused some concern for the background investigators was the beard Howard sported while at the U of W. The investigators asked every reference listed by Howard on his application, including the local gas station owner, why they thought Howard grew a beard while in college. It was as if they suspected him of being a "subversive" or a communist spy.

During his Oral Board Examination he was asked about the beard, and after a moment of thought he replied, "I was in the military when I was seventeen, shaving every day even though there was nothing there to shave. I was a firefighter after the military, and still shaving every day. Soon after becoming a full-time student, I went to the bathroom mirror, put a razor to my face, and asked myself, 'What am I doing this for?' I put the razor down and didn't shave again until applying for this job." They seemed to understand his reasoning. Next, the Oral Board challenged Howard's school interests.

After looking at his U of W transcripts, one examiner stated in a critical tone, "From the looks of your transcript, it appears that you would like to be a social worker rather than a police officer."

Howard replied without hesitation, "I would love to be a social worker, and I think that social work is what officers do."

There was a stunned silence on the board, and then one member disagreed, "Oh, no—the police officer's job is to arrest criminals and throw them in jail, and forget about it. They don't take the job personally."

Howard felt compelled to say what he truly thought, even though he feared that his chance of passing the oral exam was in serious jeopardy. Rather recklessly, and showing his newfound, and more tolerant view of the world, Howard replied, "I respectfully disagree. I believe that police officers must be concerned for the well-being of those whom they contact." Howard was surprised to learn that he passed with flying colors. He was sworn in to the SPD on November 12, 1968, and on the street after a three-day indoctrination. In those days, new SPD recruits didn't enter the training academy until a class opened. In the meantime, they were placed with experienced officers for a short time to accumulate just enough experience to fill a position for the three to five months it took to get an academy spot.

Howard was disappointed with his assignment to the Traffic Enforcement Section. *If I'm chasing speeders, how in the hell am I going to catch crooks and save the world?* he thought. It did not take long for him to learn that being in the Traffic Section allowed him to remain unburdened from routine 911 radio calls and investigations, thus affording him the opportunity to chase every emergency crime-in-progress call that came over the radio. He became even more of a hotrod than he had ever been before.

On his second day on the street, he was riding with a veteran traffic officer *(Bob Wolverton, Sr.)* when another member of their squad became involved in a high-speed chase. *Wow,* thought Howard, *This job is for me.* Bob maneuvered their car to a location the fleeing car was approaching. The officer in the chase vehicle was radioing his location, direction of travel, and reporting speeds of 60 to 70 mph. They were on a two-lane arterial street that had a parking lane on each side. Bob said, "They are approaching us now!"

The rookie's heart jumped up in his throat. He couldn't wait to join in. The fun died out a little when Bob suddenly swerved their car crossways into the oncoming lane. What made the situation even more tense was that they were only one-half block from the crest of a slight slope, with the passenger side toward the approaching projectile. Howard visualized the approaching vehicle hurtling over the crest of the hill and demolishing their car. He wanted to get out and run; but he was concerned that he would be labeled a sissy and forever disgraced. There was not much time to think about it, because only a few seconds had ticked away before the fleeing car appeared to leave the roadway as it came into view. Bob reacted instinctively—as if it were an everyday experience. He threw the police car into reverse, and it leaped backward out of the oncoming lane, just as the oncoming missile passed by, resembling just a blur to Howard. The driver had locked his brakes, causing an uncontrolled slide and spin toward an arterial cross street.

Luckily, no cars were on the cross street. Before Howard could regain his composure, Bob had stopped the police car beside the temporarily disabled quarry. Bob seemed to perform like a machine. He was instantly at the driver's door and pointing his gun at the head of the driver, yelling, "Get out of that car or I'll blow your head off." All of this happened before Howard could pull himself together and get out of the police car. He was ashamed of being so slow and awkward, but he was learning from the best. The driver managed to get the car started and sped off—challenging Bob's threat to shoot. The car chase was on again. Within a few minutes the event changed to a foot chase. The fugitive disappeared into a wooded ravine. Ten minutes had passed, when a young woman called 911 to report that the car we had been chasing was stolen from her home thirty minutes earlier. She reported that she had left her keys in the ignition.

Howard was about to learn an important investigative lesson; *never accept anything at face value.* The officer who had initiated the car chase jumped at the chance to interview the young woman. He admonished the woman, saying, "I want you to know that it is a crime to make a false crime report, and if convicted, a person could spend time in jail. We saw the person who was driving your car, and we are going to catch him. If it turns out that this is a person you know, I will personally see that you are charged with false reporting."

The woman's eyes opened wide, and her face turned pale. She replied in a shaky voice, "Ok, I don't want to lie to you. My boyfriend called me a few minutes ago and told me to call 911 and report that my car was stolen. He said that the police were looking for him." She supplied the fugitive's name, birth date, and address. This was quite a learning experience for the second day in the SPD uniform. Howard's style was aggressive, but positioning an occupied police car crossways in the path of a car chase would never be an option for him.

Because of his prior police experience, it was only a week before Howard was out chasing speeders and crooks on his own. *Without a doubt, this is the most exciting job in the world,* he thought. His expectations were confirmed, day after day.

One car chase that will never be forgotten originated in the Lake City area of Seattle. The two most significant areas of change in methods of apprehending criminals have been the use of deadly force and restrictions on high-speed vehicle pursuits. In the "old days," almost any felony suspect was fair game for drawing gunfire. High-speed vehicle pursuits were never called off, no matter how many persons were endangered. Cops would chase someone suspected of any minor crime to the end of the earth, if necessary. This incident happened very early in Howard's career. It involved both a high-speed pursuit and lots of shooting. The crime committed was only Residential Burglary. Burglary in the State of Washington was later considered a nonviolent property crime and was removed from the list of "Inherently Dangerous Crimes." Thus, in Seattle and most other cities in Washington State, officers would be severely dealt with for taking actions similar to those Howard and associates righteously used in the 60s and 70s.

Howard's unit consisted of eight one-man traffic cars. The unit would saturate a particular area of Seattle with radar cars and would work a different area every day. During each working shift, a squad meeting was held at a coffee break. On one such coffee break, they met at a restaurant in the Lake City area. The squad overheard a radio call for the district patrol units to respond to a burglary in progress at a house that was approximately eight blocks from their location.

Two males in their twenties were loading a large television into the trunk of a blue Corvair. The traffic enforcement crew reacted as most enthusiastic police officers would to such a call. They paid their bill and headed for their cars as quickly as possible. Two of the officers happened to be doubled up in one car because they had just completed a warrant arrest and had not yet picked up the other car. The heroes of this incident are the officers in that two-man car *(Doug and Larry)*.

Howard was first to arrive at the location of the burglary. He provided information via his radio to other officers that the most likely direction of travel for the blue Corvair would be northbound toward a major arterial street in Lake City. Doug and Larry responded to Howard's directions; and within minutes, they had spotted the Corvair, headed in an eastbound direction. They broadcast information that they were stopping the suspect car, which was occupied by two white males, and, coincidentally, had a television set protruding from the trunk. The car was stopped about fifty feet from an intersection, on a street adjacent to a bank parking lot. Doug got out of the police car with his gun drawn and approached the passenger side of the suspect car. Larry exited the police car to cover Doug. As Doug was nearing the rear of the suspect car, it started moving. Larry jumped back into the police vehicle and started pursuing the burglars. Much to Doug's surprise and dismay, Larry drove off without him. Frustrated, Doug ran through the adjacent bank parking lot and was standing on the sidewalk crouched with his gun pointed at the approaching suspect car after it turned the corner. The driver of the Corvair was not intimidated enough to stop. As the suspect car went by, Doug began firing at the car. Fortunately for Doug, there was a large brick wall on the opposite side of the street, and those bullets that missed the fleeing car went into the wall. Larry was so intent upon catching the suspect car that he forgot about Doug, who was anxiously waiting to be picked up by his partner. Larry flew past Doug in pursuit of the Corvair. Doug ran into the street and stopped the very next vehicle that approached him. That vehicle turned out to be a pickup truck driven by a middle-aged male. Doug said, "I'm commandeering this truck—I want you to follow that police car!"

By this time, Larry was pulling away from them at a high rate of speed. The driver of the pickup did his best as he attempted to follow the high-speed chase that was unfolding in front of him. They were flying by other traffic at speeds of up to 100 miles per hour. A couple of traffic cars from the unit intercepted them and joined the chase. The chase continued for about three miles, until the suspect car spun out as it failed to negotiate a corner in a residential area. The suspect on the passenger side immediately exited the car and ran into a yard. As Larry approached the stopped Corvair, the driver got out and made the mistake of trying to flee by crossing the street in front of the approaching police car. Later, Larry's story was that he had made a valiant effort to avoid hitting the suspect as he ran in front of the police car. Smiling slyly, Larry said that his foot must have accidentally hit the accelerator pedal as he attempted to brake to avoid him. As a result, the suspect flew off the grill of the police car, rolled over the hood, up over the top of the car, and then onto the street. Believe it or not, he got up and limped away; but he did not get far.

Doug arrived in the commandeered pickup truck a minute later. Howard also caught up with this wild, and still unfolding, incident. The other suspect was in for an additional thrill. Officers surrounded the area, and one young officer eventually sighted him in a yard. The suspect decided to continue his flight but wisely gave up when the young officer emptied his gun at him. Unbelievably, bullets struck no one.

No one followed up on how severe the judge was in sentencing those men for their crime, but there is no doubt that their experience with the cops on that day had as much or more effect on their future criminal plans as any jail sentence would have had. They could never possibly think that the value of that television set was worth the risk they had taken on that day.

If this incident had happened in the same manner fifteen years later, the officers would have been given days off without pay for the high-speed chase and "accidentally" running over the suspect; and officers who shot at the suspects would have been disciplined and retrained. Because this incident happened in the time period that it did, the officers were not criticized for their work. They received the compliments and pats on the back that officers normally received in those days when they captured criminals. Those two burglars most surely would have escaped if it were not for the aggressiveness of the officers. The officers received no more pay for the work they performed on that day than they received for a day that they did nothing more serious than writing traffic tickets.

The reality is that the lives of innocent persons have been determined to be more important than the capture of a suspect who has committed property crimes. The risk to cops and city equipment, in addition to the effort to avoid civil lawsuits, have been motivating factors in abandoning many aggressive measures when attempting to arrest crooks.

The basic law enforcement academy training began in March 1969. After an exhilarating four months of playing a role similar to a foxhound, it was difficult to adjust to the sudden calm of a classroom. To make matters worse, the military style of discipline in the academy was a nasty reminder of the Air Force boot camp nightmare. Just having to say "Sir!" before addressing the instructors was demeaning and excessive in Howard's opinion. After three years of reserve officer experience, and four months performing the duties of a Seattle Police Officer, the academy seemed a waste of time. Howard had to hide his resentment. He knew that attitude plays a big role in the success for one who faces such a challenge. He managed to survive the first half of his schooling without jeopardizing his job. He even made it through a week of firearms training, his weakest law enforcement skill.

Six of his classmates did not fare so well. They were asked to resign for various reasons, most of which were not related to academics. Howard's impression was that the instructors and administrators were eliminating academy recruits because of personality conflicts. One recruit had several years of experience with the New York City PD, and he continually let the instructors know that Seattle PD took a back seat to the NYPD. He came across as a cocky "know-it-all" in class, and he was one of the first to go. Howard became even more suspicious when the instructors would leave the classroom, telling the recruits to talk over any problems with the academy training between themselves. Coincidentally, the most vocal complainer was mysteriously dismissed from the police department. Howard was no dummy. He was convinced that the classroom was bugged, and that every word they uttered was being monitored. He quietly shared his suspicions with others.

After the firearms training, Howard was anxious to finish up the second half of the basic training so that he could get back to the fun. It was late on a Saturday night; and Howard wanted to celebrate his survival of the tough routine he had endured by treating Liz to music and dancing at a large local nightclub. The following is Howard's description of that night:

"Liz and I were invited to sit at a table with a young male acquaintance, who was alone. I ordered my fried chicken and had started on a beer, when the band started a song that was a must to dance to. Our friend Jim found a partner and joined us on the dance floor.

"After returning to our table, we found a very agitated man hovering over Jim, making threatening remarks. Apparently, he had danced with a woman for whom the irate man had possessive feelings. He wanted Jim to jump up and fight. I tried to calm the man, but he became more belligerent. We created such a disturbance that the two off-duty deputy sheriffs, who were employed by the club for security, came to our table and convinced the man to leave us alone.

"Jim said he had seen enough of that place and was going home. I watched him walk the length of the club, with the angry man following him out the front door. My caretaker instinct took over. I quickly made it to the outside stairway where Jim was cowering by the doorway, and the irate man was at the bottom of the stairway yelling terrible challenges to him.

"I suggested we reenter the club and wait for assistance from the officers. Unfortunately, there was no time for retreat, because the guy was running up the stairway at us. I jumped between the two and was successful in holding the man's arms, as I told him I was a police officer. I said that I would make sure he was charged with assault if he attacked my friend.

"Everything was going well until a large friend of the guy I was holding ran at me from my right side and caught me with a punch that broke both sides of my jaw. The blow to my jaw didn't knock me down, but I knew right away that I was in serious trouble.

"I forgot all about the guy I had been holding and grabbed the big guy to my right. We struggled violently as the jerk tried to throw me off the landing. As I was about to fall over the edge, I gathered all of my strength and threw him toward the building. The momentum of our combined 440 pounds took us through the glass entrance door with a thunderous crash, heard throughout the club. Liz told me later that from past experience she knew I was involved in something terrible when she heard the blast from the shattering glass. My sport jacket was cut to shreds by the broken door, exposing the off-duty revolver on my belt holster. I was bloody from head to toe but ended up on the floor of the lobby with a headlock on my assailant. I thought to myself, *This is serious. I had better beat on this guy a little.* I drew back my fist and smashed him in the face as hard as I could. That punch caused extreme pain to my hand. Upon checking to see what had caused the pain, I saw my little finger extending out straight beyond my closed fist. The little finger wouldn't bend because the broken glass had severed a tendon. I pleaded for help from the crowd to hold the large man until the officers could arrive, but no one would get involved. The guy finally was able to pull away from me, leaving his jacket in my hands as he ran out of the shattered doorway.

"I gave chase and found him hiding behind a car in the back parking lot. Where the strength came from was a mystery, but I nearly jerked the guy off his feet as I grabbed him by his arm and said, 'Come on, asshole, you're going to jail.' It is puzzling that he didn't resist, because I was already half dead. He could have overpowered me easily. He must have been afraid I might die, and then he would be charged with homicide. We walked back to the front of the club where officers were waiting. On-duty officers soon arrived to investigate the disaster. An aid-car crew took care of my bleeding and transported me to a hospital. Before leaving the parking lot, the investigating officers disappointed me by saying they would probably just be issuing a citation to both the men who had assaulted me, rather than booking them in the jail.

"Once at the hospital, I began worrying about my job security. *Who would believe that I was not involved in a drunken brawl?* Thinking that I most certainly would be fired, I begged the doctor to take some blood for a blood-alcohol test to prove that I had only consumed about one-half of a beer before the event began. The doctor laughed at my concern, telling me that he and the nurse knew that I was not intoxicated. He said that if it were necessary, he would be a witness to that fact.

"The next morning, bright and early, they anesthetized me and surgically installed metal hooks in my jaw. Upon waking up, and after eating some Jell-O and soup, I felt pretty good. I told the nurse I felt like going home, and she said; 'Just wait until the bands are placed on your hooks; you might change your mind.' She was right. The doctor put rubber bands on my hooks and my mouth was clamped shut. He no sooner had left the room when I panicked and screamed for a nurse to help me. This was some form of claustrophobia. I thought I was going to suffocate. They had to give me a tranquilizer, and the hospital stay was extended another day.

"My new priority in life was to master the art of getting food to my stomach through the tiny gaps between my teeth. I also had to learn to talk like a ventriloquist. Fear of losing my job, or at the very least being held back and not graduating with my class, motivated me to return to the academy after missing only one day. I went back in bandages and sling, looking like a mummy, and feeling like I had been run over by a truck. Being the laughing stock of my class was no fun, as I attempted to participate in the training programs. Soon after returning, the Training Division Commander called me to his office. I was convinced his intention was to fire me. He asked what had happened, and I did my best to mumble the entire story through my teeth. I emphasized that I had not been reckless or drinking excessively, and that I hoped my job was not in jeopardy. The captain was very good about the entire incident. He tried to ease my tension by kidding me about winning or losing the fight. He told me to keep him posted about developments of the pending criminal charges and any possible civil suits. I went back to class feeling as though my job would be salvaged.

"The criminal trial for the two jerks who had crippled me was held about three weeks later. It was devastating to hear the judge charge each of them $50 court costs while suspending a few days of jail time. Such an injustice enraged me and motivated me to sue them in civil court.

"My jaw was wired shut for a period of six weeks. My body weight dropped from 215 pounds to 165 pounds, and food was on my mind constantly for the entire six weeks. While driving by a fast food hamburger restaurant, the smell drove me wild. I stopped and ordered the greasiest hamburger with "the works" on it and then rushed home and threw it into the food blender with a half can of tomato sauce. I greedily drank my hamburger. The broken jaw caused so much misery that I decided I would not seek revenge beyond a lawsuit in this instance, but I would certainly kill the next person who might break my jaw.

"It took about a year to settle the civil case, and we finally settled for a $1000 judgment from each man. I accepted a beat-up convertible from one man, and the other man owned nothing. I was never able to collect a thing from him; and after he committed suicide, I had to sign a release of my lien so that his estate could be settled. The friend, whom I had defended, came out of the incident without a scratch. He visited me in the hospital one time and thanked me, but I have not heard from him since.

"The suffering caused by the broken jaw was a reminder throughout my career to never assume that because I'm on the "side of right" *(like the Lone Ranger)* justice will prevail in my favor. There is no question that, although I was the hero in this story, I was the big loser."

The last half of Howard's basic training was more difficult than the first half. He struggled to participate in class discussions by mumbling through his wired gums. He graduated with his jaw still wired shut and gives much credit to his forced silence in the class. He would not have been able to "mouth off" in class if he had wanted to.

By this time in his life, Howard defined himself as a "risk taker," and he was well aware that it was only fate that had allowed him to survive those incidents that could have so easily taken his life. The broken jaw incident was a tough one. He realized that he could have been sliced up more severely than he had been when he crashed through the plate-glass entryway to the nightclub. As bad as it was, he never considered the assault as one of his near-death experiences. Howard was ready to move on to bigger and better adventures.

CHAPTER 5

Back to Traffic Enforcement

Just before academy graduation in late 1969, the recruits were asked to declare their preferred assignment. There were openings in the Traffic Section, and that was Howard's first choice. After experiencing the freedom to chase crooks that the traffic assignment had afforded him, he couldn't resist going back. What thrilled him even more was that the Traffic Section was one of the few units in the SPD that was scheduled to be equipped with the boxy-looking 1970 Plymouth Satellite. That car sported a 440-cubic-inch engine, and it handled better at high speed than any car Howard would drive in his lifetime. He always wondered why Plymouth changed the design of a car that performed like the 70 Satellite after only one year. Howard made the most of the two years that he was privileged to race around in such a magnificent hotrod. Not one high-speed chase was lost in Seattle when the Satellite was involved.

He first realized the Satellite's capability one evening during a traffic stop on Rainier Avenue South near South Henderson Street. Howard was at the driver's door of a speeder when a carload of kids threw a beer bottle at him. Luckily, the bottle shattered at his feet. The speeder was told to get on his way, and Howard ran for his car. He could hear the engine rev up on the car occupied by the kids, and he knew that the chase was on. They had at least a three-block head start. They turned right, traveling eastbound on Henderson Street. The Satellite leaped from the curb and accelerated like a bullet to close the gap to less than a block as they approached a "T" intersection with a stop sign. *(Seward Park Avenue South)* The kids ran the stop sign and nearly skidded out of control making a right turn. Howard realized he was approaching the intersection far too rapidly to negotiate the hard right turn. He was convinced his reckless abandon would cost him this time, and that he would certainly lose control and crash. The car literally amazed Howard as it completed the sharp right turn without breaking traction and accelerated out of the turn nearly on the bumper of the fleeing car. After evaluating the competition, the renegade driver quickly gave up the chase. He was subjected to a boring lecture, and two minor tickets for "Throwing Debris From a Vehicle" and a "Stop Sign" violation. Howard was so surprised and delighted with the Satellite's performance, he couldn't get mad at the kids.

There were to be many more examples of the 70 Satellite's capability. One exceptionally wild chase remains most vivid in Howard's memory. Larry, a close friend in his squad, initiated a high-speed chase involving a stolen jeep with a modified engine. Soon Howard and another friend, Jerry, joined Larry. All three were driving 1970 Satellites. They started in the North End but were soon on Interstate 5 at speeds up to 120 mph. Howard was third in line, so he had a good view of the amazing driving going on a block ahead of him. On the Canal Bridge, Larry rammed the rear of the Jeep a couple of times, but the driver was not deterred. They exited the freeway in South Seattle, still traveling at speeds of 60 to 100 mph. The driver of the fleeing jeep then took to the side streets.

This would usually be considered an indication that the driver and his three young passengers were looking for a place to bail out and get lost. Jerry had maneuvered his car close behind the Jeep; and as it started a fast left turn, Jerry rammed the left side of the rear fender. This caused the rear of the Jeep to go airborne, and it rolled end-over-end in the intersection. By this time, there were many South Precinct patrol units nearby. The officers expected to be treating the four occupants for serious injuries. Instead, the four popped out of the open-sided Jeep and ran. It did not take long to round them up. None of the fortunate car thieves were injured. The Jeep did not fare as well.

On another evening, Howard was working radar at the approach to the Alaskan Way Viaduct. It was pretty boring until the sounder on the radar unit gave off a high-pitched squeal. This was very different from the usual low-pitch groan given off by cars traveling at normal speeds. The pointer on the speed indicator jumped up to 85 mph. The fight for his life that this traffic stop led to is presented here in Howard's own words:

"I was working in a radar car, monitoring a 35-mph zone that preceded a raised viaduct where the speed limit increases to 50 mph. I knew that I was going to get a "hot" reading when I noticed a car approaching that looked as if it were getting ready to become airborne. I obtained a radar reading of 85 mph on the car. The motorist didn't notice me as he sped by, so I got a thrill ride attempting to catch up with him. After a one-mile pursuit, I was able to stop him on the raised portion of the viaduct.

"As I exited the radar car and walked toward the viaduct railing, the motorist met me. I looked him over carefully to make sure that he wasn't hostile or insane. He seemed pretty normal looking to me. As we were stopping, he threw what appeared to be a six-pack of beer into the back seat. While we talked, it became evident that he had been consuming alcoholic beverages.

"From his speech and his physical ability, he did not appear to be too intoxicated to drive. I decided to write a Reckless Driving ticket and allow the man to go on his way. I told him he could have a seat in his car, and I would be right with him. I went to sit in the radar car and noticed that the man was approaching the passenger door of the police car. As I rolled the passenger window down a little to see what he wanted, he reached in the window, unlocked the door, and slid into the passenger seat beside me. Needless to say, I was a little put out. I told the man to get out of the police car until I had finished his citation. He said, 'No, I want to see what you are doing.' I told him I would not allow him to sit in the police vehicle, but he insisted he was going to stay. Fortunately, I had called for a backup unit because of the extreme speed involved.

"Now there was a realization that I might have misjudged the sobriety of my traffic violator. It was evident that this man's judgment was seriously affected by the alcohol he had consumed, even though his physical ability seemed adequate. I told him, 'Because of the way you were driving, and are now acting, I am concerned that you have had too much beer to drink to be driving.'

"'I haven't been drinking any beer, and you couldn't prove it if I had,' he answered.

"I shot back, 'Well, if you haven't been drinking any beer, what was that you threw into your back seat when you were stopping here?'

"He mumbled, 'You didn't see me throw anything into my back seat.'

"When Larry *(my backup unit)* arrived, I asked him to look into the back window of the man's car to see what he had thrown there. As Larry approached the car, the motorist bolted from my car and was about to jump on the Larry's back, when I caught up and grabbed him. He struggled, and we went to the pavement. We rolled around on the roadway in front of the radar car, with 50-mph traffic passing by within a few feet of us. I gradually forced the man up against the guardrail of the viaduct, and I squeezed him hard against the railing—not wanting to roll around near that fast traffic anymore. The man started screaming that I was breaking his back on the railing. I told him that I would let up on the pressure if he would quit fighting. He agreed, and as soon as I loosened my grip on the railing, he lifted me off the pavement and nearly had me over the railing. While off my feet and looking down at railroad tracks forty feet below, it was like staring certain death right in the face. Extraordinary strength sparked by intense fear, plus my 220-pound body weight, saved me from a long fall. The motorist and I went squirming to the pavement like a couple of vicious dogs. Poor Larry was frustrated because he couldn't find a place to grab the guy. I finally ended up on top of the motorist, as he lay face down on the roadway. I took a handful of the man's hair and pulled his head up as far as his neck would bend backwards. I said, 'Now, asshole—one more move and I'll squash your face!' *(Other profane utterances have been omitted.)* I was pissed off and tired. I meant what I had said, and I guess he believed me. We were able to handcuff the man without further problems.

"Just as we got the guy to his feet, my sergeant showed up, and the handcuffed man started looking for pity. He began crying and complaining that I hurt his back, and that I had kicked him in the back. Before my sergeant even asked me what had happened, or why my police hat was down on the railroad tracks below the viaduct, he looked at me very seriously and asked accusingly, 'Did you kick him in the back?' If you think I was pissed off before the sergeant arrived, imagine how I felt after that stupid question.

"I answered, 'No, I didn't kick him in the back, but I sure as shit should have.' I was outraged that my sergeant would even ask that question of me after the ordeal that I had just experienced. The sergeant continued to press the issue of possible excessive physical force on my part, and I continued to become more upset and defensive.

"The driver was charged with DUI, Reckless Driving, and Resisting Arrest. He was lucky it wasn't Homicide *(and so was I)*. He could have driven away after signing a citation for Reckless Driving, if he had been able to control his emotions. That man came to court and pled guilty to all three charges. He shook my hand and sincerely apologized to me for his actions on that terrible day. I was totally astonished by his change of attitude. Apparently, alcohol gave him a Dr. Jekyl/Mr.Hyde personality. The sergeant played a small part in this drama, but he placed me in a position of having to defend my actions, when he should have been treating me as a victim. This is also an example of how a relatively minor traffic incident can be escalated to a life-or-death situation. I never forgot the sergeant's lack of support and his ignorance regarding that situation."

By this time, Howard was convinced that he was living a special life as an exceptionally privileged person. This was the fifth time that he could have just as well been killed, rather than surviving to tell this story.

Although Howard had no experience with motorcycles, most of the officers in the Traffic Section were on a long waiting list to be assigned to the two-wheelers. The job sounded exciting, so Howard put his name on the list. He went through a rigorous training course on the Harley Davidson 74 *(The Hog)* and did pretty well. He was assigned to police motorcycles in 1971.

CHAPTER 6

Temptation and Corruption

The late 1960s and early 1970s were times of very high morale in the Seattle Police Department. The officers had survived a period of reform, and corruption in the department had been eliminated. *(Yes, eliminated!)* Those who were being investigated for past corruption were the only cops who were not comfortable. Many retired earlier than they had planned. The system of graft, which had plagued most large police departments, had seriously affected the quality of performance of a small percentage of officers. The Seattle Police Department recovered and became a very aggressive and effective law enforcement agency.

Imagine a rookie cop in the early 1960s being assigned to an old-timer on a downtown beat. The new kid would be idealistic, with preconceived notions about becoming a "supercop," and wanting to save society from the criminal element. In the days when some cops were taking graft, the crooked old beat cop would first introduce the rookie to the back room at the local bar. A couple of free shots of booze would slow the rookie down a little. The rookie would then have to tag along as the old cop made his rounds. Some of the stops would be for free cigarettes, more booze, free food, and/or plain envelopes containing money.

The old cop would explain that they were underpaid and that taking money and gifts was a way of supplementing their income *(a necessary evil)*. The rookie who got caught up in the corruption learned fast; to remain healthy and keep his job, he had to either participate in the system, or at least keep his mouth shut.

For those officers, police work became secondary to personal business. Police payoffs caused officers to get their priorities confused. As soon as an officer takes illegal money, he/she becomes a part of the criminal society that he/she has taken an oath to combat. From that time on, an officer can no longer put his/her heart into aggressively pursuing criminals because the officer has joined their ranks.

Fortunately for the taxpayers, an out-of-town police chief was hired in the 1960s to clean up the department. The Chief was very unpopular with the rank and file, but he was successful in his efforts. Police payoffs became a thing of the past. Cops now could concentrate on doing their job.

This significant change in the police department was still in progress when Howard joined the force. There were some hangers-on, left over from the contamination of corruption within the department, who not only couldn't care less about law enforcement, but also resented those like Howard, who lived for their work. Still, there were more subtle forms of favors offered to police officers. During his first assignment, as a fresh rookie, officers in his squad made it a point to show him which restaurants offered free or half-priced meals. This was not considered a form of graft that was part of the ongoing crackdown. Until a new chief issued a policy order that prohibited officers from accepting so much as a free cup of coffee, the free meals were an acceptable benefit. Even so, Howard avoided the restaurants that refused money from officers. He reluctantly patronized those that charged half price for the food, but he left a good tip. The justification was that at least the restaurant would not lose money by feeding him. It was a relief when the order came down that paying less than full price was unacceptable.

It is important to note that not all of the cops were dishonest in those bad years. The vast majority of police officers were honest and hard-working professionals. It was the dishonest cops who had marred the image of the profession.

Change in any profession is usually met with resistance, and change causes a certain amount of stress and morale problems. Veteran officers sometimes wax nostalgic and speak of how great it was to be a cop in "the good old days." They complain, "That's when cops were real cops, rather than social workers."

Howard's old partner, Jerry Hofstee, told the rookies who complained about policy and procedure changes, "Enjoy yourselves now, because you are now experiencing what you will eventually refer to as your 'good old days.'" In Howard's "good old days," officers were enthusiastically pursuing criminals, and they believed that the public and the administration wanted them to be aggressive. There was seldom a shortage of police officers to respond to a call. When the public needed a cop and the call was dispatched, officers had to worry about running over each other racing to the call. Each competed to get to a call ahead of the others. No matter how many limitations were placed upon the pursuit of criminals, and despite occasional lack of support from the police administration, the justice system, and other segments of society, Howard's enthusiasm for police work was never dampened.

Howard believed he was well aware of the danger involved in his newly chosen profession. One element of danger that had never occurred to him was that of the alluring invitations to stray from ethical and professional performance. Being an honest cop was not always easy. The reason the public periodically hears of police officers being investigated for abuse of authority is because the temptations are great, and they are plentiful. Not only are officers placed in positions where money and valuable property falls into their care at death scenes and crime scenes, there are always people around who want to give officers things, for favors in return. The temptation least talked about is the opportunity for sexual encounters.

One temptress that Howard never forgot was a pretty woman in her twenties whom he met as a result of a traffic violation. While working at a Kingdome event on a very recognizable police motorcycle, he had come to a complete stop at a traffic signal that had just turned red. A car sped on by him in the lane to his right. His first thought was that it must be a DUI, because no sober person would run a red light where a motorcycle cop was stopped. The emergency lights and siren were actuated, and the errant driver pulled over within a block. Before Howard could get his kickstand down, a gorgeous young woman exited her car and approached him. Her miniskirt accentuated a pair of legs that were too perfect to be real. She had a body that resembled a 60s-era Barbie Doll that had come to life. Taken aback by her gorgeous face, which bore a striking resemblance to a young Elizabeth Taylor, Howard muttered, "Do you realize that the signal was red at Atlantic Street when you went through, and I was stopped next to the lane you were in?"

With a comfortable smile, and showing no sign of worry, she answered, "Yes, officer, I knew the light had turned red; and I saw you there. I went through the red signal purposely so that I could meet you." Howard was not a bad looking guy, but he knew he was far from irresistible. He had heard of police groupies, but the surprised cop never had a personal experience with anyone like this. One idea that ran through his mind was that the woman messed up and ran the light, and this was her way of talking him out of writing a ticket. He always said that no one could talk him out of a ticket that was deserved, except his mother *(maybe!)*.

Taking a deep breath, Howard said, "That is very friendly of you, but I need to see your driver's license."

"What for, officer?"

"You ran the red light—I write tickets to people who run red lights, even though you are a very nice person," was his reply.

She dug her license from her purse, and with a smile that would melt the toughest and meanest of cops, said, "Well, if I'm going to get a ticket, it will be a pleasure getting it from you." Now Howard was wishing he were somewhere else. He was feeling like an idiot, standing there on the sidewalk and writing a traffic citation to someone who obviously was nuts about him— especially while she was telling him that she had a particular fascination for police officers; and that she was very lonely while her Merchant Marine husband was out at sea. He completed the citation, and she thanked him before she drove off. His feelings were mixed. First, there was fear that someone like this could falsely accuse him of writing her a ticket for rejecting his advances; second, he felt like a jerk for having to write such a pleasant person a ticket. Howard would run into this same woman again one evening a year later, while working Patrol for one month of temporary duty, as part of an exchange program between the Traffic Section and the Patrol Division.

During what had been a quiet, uneventful shift, two women passed Howard and his partner, honking their horn and waving wildly for them to pull the patrol car over. They pulled into a restaurant parking lot and his partner rolled his window down to talk to them. It was the same woman he had met at the red signal near the Kingdome. They asked the officers if they had time to have coffee with them in the restaurant. His partner lied and told them they were on a call and had been pretty busy all evening. After the women left, Howard told his story about the previous meeting with the beautiful woman. The partner told Howard that the flirtatious woman lived in that area of town. He said that she and her girlfriend went out cruising for cops all the time, and that they were "police groupies." Howard asked if any of the officers ever took them up on their offer. He answered that some did, but most were pretty leery of them. Howard made a bet that she was not looking for a boyfriend, she was just keeping score.

Then there was the time that Howard and Jerry Hofstee were in the downtown area looking for a bank robber. A call came in from the Camlin Hotel that a maid had found a large amount of money in a room she cleaned. The two motorcycle officers were the first to arrive. They were told that the occupants of the room were not there, but they still used care in entering. There was money all over the room—packs of large bills overflowing from drawers in the desk and dresser. Their first fear was, "Is this the money from the bank robbery three blocks away? And if so, where is the robber?" Their second fear was, "Who is going to believe that we did not pocket some of this cash?" The officers looked under the bed and in the closet, and then backed out of the room as if someone had died of the plague in there. They maintained a guard on the room until robbery detectives arrived. That did not end their worries. Next they were concerned that they would be blamed if the maid, the detectives, or anyone else had pilfered money out of the room. A day of worry was for nothing. The money remained intact throughout the investigation. It was not the proceeds from the bank robbery. It seems that a high-level drug deal was about to take place, and the maid had not received the request from the occupants of the room for no room service. The money was seized, and no one ever claimed a penny of it.

In the late 70s, Howard and Jerry received a true test of placing their ethics over and above their loyalty to other officers. The incident was a blow to their morale, caused by the shocking reality of knowing two cops who were arrested for committing burglaries while on duty.

The two motorcycle cops worked closely with the Seattle Traffic Engineering employees who arranged traffic control equipment around the Kingdome area for events. One day, an engineering employee cornered the officers, seeking their reaction to what his crew had observed cops doing. The engineering crew had been picking up traffic signs after an evening event; and at 1:00 a.m., they heard a burglary alarm sounding on a warehouse in the industrial area. When they checked to see if police had been called, they experienced a big surprise. Not only were cops at the warehouse, two cops were loading items from the warehouse into a plain city car that was occupied by a sergeant in uniform.

Both Howard and his partner were shocked; and they hoped that whatever these guys had seen was legitimate, but they feared the worst. The first thing that Howard asked the engineering employees is if they reported what they had seen. They said that they described what they had seen to their supervisors, and the police department had been advised. Howard checked some resources inside the police department; and he was able to confirm that the matter had been reported and was being investigated. There was no hesitation in his decision to investigate the possible criminal activity within the police ranks, but it was a painful and stressful experience.

Not long after, Howard was shocked to read a news report that two district patrol officers *(veterans of eighteen and twenty years)* had been arrested for burglary in the industrial area. He was sickened. These were officers whom he had worked with when the motorcycle units were assigned to the Kingdome events. Previously, Howard suspected that they had lost their enthusiasm for police work by the lackadaisical way that they responded to assignments by police radio; but he never would have dreamed that they had accumulated so much disrespect for their profession.

Howard was exceedingly astonished when he discovered details of the events that led to the arrest. A former police academy classmate, Jim, who had dropped out of the academy to later become a railroad detective, was invited to assist the two errant officers in burglaries of warehouses on railroad property. They wanted him to open up the buildings and shut off alarms for them so that they could loot the buildings at will. How they had guts enough, or why they were nuts enough, to ask such a thing of someone is beyond comprehension. Jim was afraid to tell them no, and he said he would think it over. He confided in a friend and former academy classmate who had retired on a medical disability. They made the decision to report the proposition to the administration of the police department. The problem was that the railroad detective was familiar with the camaraderie within the police department in the 1970s that had carried over from the 50s and 60s. He feared that he would be killed if he reported the criminals; and he feared that he would be killed if he joined them, or if he didn't join them in their criminal activity.

There was one particular commander, whose credibility and whose desire for a corruption-free department was recognized above all others. Jim gathered his courage and reluctantly went to that commander with his story. The plan was for the detective to agree to help the patrol officers plan a burglary. He would open a warehouse for them and ensure that there were no interruptions from railroad employees. The commander would have police units waiting for the patrol officers to load stolen items into their police car and then arrest them. This was a good plan, but Jim was suspicious and feared that he would become a scapegoat for the police department. He believed that he would be set up to look as if he were the burglar, and killed by the police, thus making the police look like heroes and eliminating him as a witness against them. This sounds far fetched, but for those who are intimately familiar with sporadic law-enforcement cronyism of the 50s and 60s, maybe not too far fetched. Another shocking coincidence that Howard would later be made aware of is that the retired academy classmate, Mike, had offered his assistance and advice to Jim. Mike assured Jim that he would position himself strategically, so that he could fire upon any officer who posed a threat to Jim. *(Whew!!)* The burglary was planned. The commander didn't doublecross the railroad detective. The officers were arrested, and convicted— and they served time!!!

It is difficult to describe just how adversely this event had affected Howard. He felt sorry for the officers—he was mad at the officers—he was shocked—he was disappointed—he was embarrassed—he was disgusted. Jim's life was thrown into turmoil. He believed that any Seattle Police Officer might someday take revenge. He even mistrusted Howard. Howard personalized the entire matter, trying to analyze what caused this tragedy. It was evident that the officers had not profited greatly. They were stealing "junk." The only reasonable solution is that they were suffering burnout. They committed career suicide. The old veteran officers are not the only cops that can be led astray.

There are continual reminders in the media that no matter how strict and careful a police administration may be regarding misconduct, there will always be officers who give in to temptation. Two cases in the nineties, involving officers whose integrity Howard would have staked his reputation on, made the local news as a result of criminal acts. One was a DUI Squad officer who was taking his arrested drunks to a cash machine so that they could pay him up front to let them go. He could justify his criminal actions by considering what he did to the DUI drivers was no worse than the drivers having to pay a fine to the court. It was a bargain compared to what they saved in court costs, attorney's fees, and elevated insurance premiums. The DUI Squad officer was operating profitably, because most DUIs were quite happy to give him a hundred or two just to avoid the court. However, he eventually ran into a bitter customer who turned him in.

Another acquaintance in the department contacted a prostitute in his district about a warrant for her arrest. He was gracious enough to ignore the warrant in return for sexual favors. That extortion worked well for a while, but she tired of his blackmail scheme and set him up for an Internal Investigation Unit sting. The newspapers were delighted to tell the story of both officers. Naturally, they were both fired. These were intelligent officers, with promising careers ahead of them; yet, their resistance to temptation was low, and they were induced to commit criminal acts.

The law enforcement profession will continue to attract media attention directed at cops who misuse and/or abuse the tremendous authority with which they are entrusted. Those few cops who weaken, and give in to one or more of the many temptations designed to lure them into unprofessional or criminal behavior, cause the public to judge the entire profession by the abhorrent acts of a few. Nothing is more demoralizing for the honest cops than to read about, or personally experience, fellow officers going bad. Such acts tend to play right into the hands of those detractors of the law enforcement profession who hate, fear, or resent authority. Howard most certainly was not attracted to law enforcement to see how much money he could earn. On many occasions, he joked that he would do the job free of charge. In fact, he had done exactly that, when as a young man just out of the military, he performed police duties for three years as a reserve deputy sheriff, without compensation. Howard loved to work with people, and craved the excitement of chasing and capturing criminals. He considered his assignment to motorcycles as "heaven sent." Almost "sent to heaven" was what the assignment turned out to be.

Howard A. Monta on his police Harley 'Hog' in 1977.

CHAPTER 7

Police Motorcycles

Howard's philosophy about catching criminals had always been that a cop does not have to possess extraordinary talent to make memorable arrests. All that is required is a little luck and a lot of desire on the part of the cop. One night in the 70s, Howard engaged in a foot chase with a young man who had been stripping a motorcycle on a dark side street. Howard was wearing a leather police motorcycle jacket and about twenty pounds of police equipment. Several blocks and many fences later, Howard jumped on him as the teenager tripped after crashing into a yard. The first words out of the kid's mouth were, "How did an old guy like you catch me? Last year I was on the Lake Sammamish track team!" Howard was only thirty-five, and he was taken aback by the "old guy" comment.

Without thinking, Howard responded, "Well, you had fear, youth, and speed going for you, but I had a whole lot of desire going for me." His theory was that if you remain alert and place yourself in a location where there is a chance of making contact with a criminal—with a little luck, the crook will find you. Many criminals who are captured in the act of committing their deed or during their flight are captured because of their own stupidity and lack of planning. However, even when brilliant-minded criminals who have meticulously planned for success challenge the justice system, their bad luck sometimes becomes an overriding factor in their demise. Crooks are also subject to "Murphy's Law": "If anything can go wrong, it will" *(Edward A. Murphy, "Success & Failure")*, and it is surprising that so many intelligent criminals stumble into the grasp of cops.

The Harley Davidson 74, equipped with saddlebags, storage box with emergency light on the lid, and a windshield, was not the fastest motorcycle on the street; but it sure was prestigious. Even though it was a cumbersome machine, with a top speed of just a little over 80-mph, the hog could outmaneuver any car—but couldn't outrun a Volkswagen! In downtown traffic, you could easily take it the wrong way on a one-way street in heavy traffic and use the sidewalks when all else failed. Crooks did not have a chance to escape such a magnificent law enforcement tool. Howard was amused when one admiring teenager told him, "Man, what a scooter. I'll bet no one would ever try to outrun one of those babies!"

Not wanting to give the kid any ideas, Howard replied, "Yeah, it's a hot one—it'll do over a hundred. Nobody gets away from me."

For a short period of time, Howard was assigned to the downtown district. He caught so many parking meter looters, shoplifters, and purse-snatchers that he became bored with the work. On one occasion, he did not have to get off the motorcycle to apprehend a meter looter. The suspect spotted the police motorcycle and fled on foot. Howard followed for blocks to tire the thief. That makes the thief easier to catch when the officer decides it is time to leave the motorcycle and pursue on foot. Near the end of the chase, Howard took the huge motorcycle onto the sidewalk only a few feet behind the man, and yelled, "I'm going to run this motorcycle right up your back." That caused the tired thief to dodge into a narrow entryway to a building. Howard had the Hog right on his butt, preventing him from opening the door. If he got off the motorcycle, he knew the thief would run again. Howard decided to stay on the bike and keep the suspect pinned against the door until other units arrived. The unusual scene in the doorway amused onlookers and arriving officers. Lots of change, and a counterfeit parking meter key, was taken from the suspect's pockets.

Chasing petty thieves was great sport, but Howard desired the ultimate thrill of catching robbers, rapists, and murderers. When police officers focus their full attention on catching crooks, anything can be accomplished. This motorcycle cop continually placed himself where dangerous criminals were known to be, or where he anticipated they might be. Many important arrests were the result of his planning and tenacity. The following stories represent only a fraction of the exciting and dangerous adventures enjoyed by Howard during his 15-year assignment to motorcycles.

Armed Robber Gets A Free Pass. Cops are always at a disadvantage when chasing a criminal. The restrictions on the use of deadly force are very strict; yet the criminals acknowledge no rules. The following story illustrates how vulnerable Howard was while chasing an armed robber who turned out to be an escapee from an Oregon penitentiary. Note the shocking lack of justice that occurred after the cop risked it all to catch the desperate crook.

In 1973, while working in a high-crime area of Seattle, Howard responded to the armed robbery of a shoe store. A robber had shoved a cocked and loaded pistol into the face of an elderly storeowner. The brave young robber got away with a grand total of $12 for his valiant effort. The description of the robber was as follows: white male, twenty, blond hair, blue jacket, and blue jeans. As it turned out, this clown's wife was supposed to circle the block in their station wagon and pick him up after the big heist. There were so many police units in the area that she must have panicked and fled, leaving the hero without a ride.

About six to eight blocks from the robbery, Howard noticed a blond, white male matching the broadcast description, with the exception of his jacket, which was white. He was walking away from Howard's location, across a busy arterial. There was something funny about the man's jacket. It was kind of fuzzy, and it had blue trim. He asked himself, *Could this be a blue jacket turned inside out?* Howard attempted to transmit a message to the radio operator that he was observing a possible sus-

71

pect in the armed robbery, but the radio operator was broad-casting the following: "—and here is radio with another recap of the description of the armed robbery of the shoe store located at—," and he went on and on with the broadcast.

Meanwhile, the suspect had turned, looked at the excited cop, and started climbing up a rock embankment into a yard. It was obvious that Howard wouldn't be able to get his message to radio, and in those days, portable radios were not available. He followed the suspect into the yard, while trying to act cool and dumb. So as not to alarm the suspect, he said, "Just a minute, sir. I would like to talk to you." The suspect looked at the anxious cop once more and ran like a rabbit between the houses. The chase was on. When the suspect went over the first fence, which was about four feet high, it was obvious that he was wearing a blue jacket that had been reversed.

There was no longer any doubt that this man was the robber. They both vaulted the first fence like it wasn't even there. Howard was close behind, running across a large, open field. The suspect was the slimmer of the two, and he wore tennis shoes. Howard wore high boots that are designed for riding on a police motorcycle—certainly not for running. The robber was gaining ground. Howard tried to induce him to stop by shouting, "Stop, or I'll blow your fucking head off!" The message had no effect on him, except maybe to make him run faster. There were plenty of cops around, but none of them knew a suspect was being chased and that a fellow officer was in serious danger. There was no one in the area to ask for help. It was like being in a ghost town. He knew then that if he shot this guy in the back, he would be second-guessed forever; however, the guy could shoot him any time he wished to, especially after leaping over any of the many fences they scaled.

Even though warning shots were illegal, it was not illegal to discharge a firearm to summon help in an emergency. While still running as fast as he could, and yelling threats at the fleeing criminal, Howard pointed his revolver as straight up in the air as possible and let a round fly. It made a lot of noise, and it inspired the suspect to run faster. He scaled a six-foot fence and quickly disappeared from sight. They had traveled about two blocks and over six fences, and now Howard had lost sight of the guy who posed a very serious threat to his health.

He started knocking on doors and windows to get attention. When people finally started appearing, he screamed to them to call for help. While searching the back yards, the blue jacket was found near a huge fence. A man and woman were standing in an adjacent yard pointing toward a nearby house. The gunshot was getting some attention. Howard noticed a slight movement behind a chimney on the side of the house and realized that his life was in great jeopardy. It was apparent that the man he had been chasing could see Howard, but Howard couldn't see him. The frightened cop crouched and was ready to empty his gun at any movement. He fixed his gun sights on the chimney where he had noticed the movement and screamed, "Let me see those hands empty, or you're a dead man!" Much to his relief, he saw two empty hands extend out from behind the chimney. The man was placed spread-eagled on the ground and handcuffed. As Howard walked the robber out from between the houses to the street, a police helicopter flew low overhead. It was a welcome sight.

Two or three police cars came roaring up. There was no longer that isolated feeling that had so disturbed him while he pursued the robber. He was on an emotional high, though exhausted. Howard had captured his first armed robber. He was also puzzled. Why didn't this man, who turned out to be a prison escapee, shoot Howard when he had his golden opportunity? He was about to find out why.

While Howard was busy trying to catch his breath, an aggressive young officer was asking the robber where his gun was. When the suspect said nothing, the officer grabbed him by the collar and got in his face. The robber must have had previous experience with cops who have no patience for criminals. Without hesitation, the robber told them that he had lost the gun out of his waistband as he went over the first fence. If he hadn't lost the gun, Howard would probably not have survived to share this story. It was devastatingly disappointing to find out that this dangerous man, whom he had risked his life to apprehend, would not be charged with the crime. The prosecutor must have determined it was not worth the expense to take him to trial and incarcerate him in Washington State, when he was wanted for escaping the state prison in Oregon. The morale of all the officers involved was lowered when the lowlife was sent back to Oregon.

Motorcycle Cop Catches Murderer. Here is Howard's version of an arrest of a murder suspect that was simply the result of being in the right place at the right time:

"I was the first police unit to arrive at a call concerning 'gunfire with a man down' in one of Seattle's low-income housing projects. A man was lying in a yard, and he didn't appear to be in very good shape. It was a relief to see a fire department aid unit arriving in the area behind me. A person in the gathering crowd said, 'You might like to talk to that woman down the street there. She might know something about this.' There was a large female walking away, about two blocks down the street. Any masterful investigator would have acted upon such a lead.

"It was explained to the woman *(Leola)* that a witness thought she might know something about the shooting. She mumbled, 'He was leaving with suitcases.' She also said something about, '—that other woman.' When asked if she had any weapons on her person, she said, 'I throwed it under the house over there.'

"'What did you throw under the house?'

"'The gun.'

"'Before I go crawling around looking for a gun, I'd better check your purse for weapons.'

"'There isn't anything but money and a checkbook in there.'

"'I need to check anyway.'

"She held the purse out, and in plain sight was a small black 22-caliber revolver with a pearl handle. When asked if that was the gun that she had said she had thrown under the house, she said that it was. One might wonder what would have happened if I had not been cautious about looking in her purse— if instead I had looked under the house while she stood behind me. Would she have shot me in the back and made her escape?

"The motive for this homicide was that Leola's common-law husband was about to leave town with a mistress. She had purchased a gun from a pawnshop about two weeks earlier. Her excuse for the purchase of the gun was that the victim had been calling and threatening her. Leola took a cab to where she found the husband loading suitcases into his car. She claimed that he grabbed her by the arm and tried to push her to the ground, and in fear, she took the gun out of her purse and it fired accidentally. However, eyewitnesses to the shooting told detectives that Leola had the gun in her hand just after she left the cab. If the gun had gone off accidentally, then it went off three times accidentally, because three shots had been fired. Leola was charged and convicted of Second-Degree Murder, and she was committed to the Purdy Treatment Center For Women in Gig Harbor, WA in July 1972. The problem is that Leola served her time, and she is out now; but her common-law husband is still dead."

An appropriate title for Howard's next adventure is **"Robber Gets Life Sentence – Life Didn't Mean 'Life.'"** This is a story about an armed robber who should never be allowed to see the light of day outside of a secure prison facility. Society should have ensured he was not given the opportunity to continue victimizing innocent persons. You will agree when you read this miscreant's criminal history. His first name is Curtis. Of course, he has a number of aliases. After telling of the miraculous capture of the elusive Curtis, this miscreant's criminal history will be reviewed; and then Howard's disappointment with the justice system's handling of this arrest will be shared. Howard's own version of his luck and fate while encountering this dangerous criminal is as follows:

"This robbery incident dates back to October 24, 1977. The robbery of Cleo's Apparel, a women's clothing store on Rainier Avenue South, in Seattle, was masterminded by two brave men, Curtis and James. Before making their getaway, Curtis struck one of the women clerks on the head with a large automatic pistol.

"I happened to be in the area on a police motorcycle when SPD radio broadcast that two black male suspects had fled the store in an eastbound direction. That was the only description of the suspects that was given, and there was no description of a vehicle as yet. I knew that other police units would be responding on the main arterial streets, so I decided to approach on a side street to the east of the store. Not even a full minute had passed when a 1970 Ford Thunderbird entered the arterial that I was on, without stopping for the stop sign. Having no further information about the robbers, my suspicion of the Ford was strengthened because it was occupied by two black males and the driver seemed to be in a big hurry. Also, the Ford was an appropriate distance from the robbery for the time that had elapsed. I followed the Thunderbird on a side street, with my emergency lights on, and attempted to tell our busy radio operator what I was doing.

"The two male occupants of the car appeared to be trying to conceal something around the front seat. The car made a fast right turn on to a dead end street, stopping in the private driveway of a residence. Both the driver and passenger exited the car. At this time, I still had not received a physical or clothing description of the robbery suspects. I didn't feel that I was justified in taking my gun out of the holster yet. This fact left me in a very stressful situation.

"I told the passenger to remain inside the car while I talked to the driver; however, he continued walking away. The driver presented a Washington State driver's license and nervously stated that he was in a hurry to pick up an injured relative and take the relative to a hospital. The passenger, Curtis, continued walking around to the front of the house where they were parked. I yelled at him to return to the car. Curtis responded by saying that he had to see if his cousin was at home. He continued walking out of my sight around the side of the house.

"As backup police units arrived, I received information from radio that the robbery suspects had used a light blue, late model car to make their getaway. I was also informed that the money from the robbery was taken in a pink paper bag. The Thunderbird certainly matched the description, and through the open door of the car I observed a pink paper bag, with a dark suede jacket wrapped around it, lying on the driver's seat.

"The driver was placed under arrest for suspicion of robbery, and Miranda rights were read to him. By this time other units had the entire block surrounded. There was a large caliber automatic pistol underneath the passenger seat of the car. The money from the robbery was in the pink paper bag on the car seat. I was feeling pretty good about finding the robbery vehicle, and about the arrest of one suspect, but I was disheartened about losing track of the second suspect. Several officers searched the entire block where Curtis was last seen walking around the corner of the house. After about half an hour of searching, the police units had given up and were being relieved from the scene. I felt so bad about losing Curtis that I asked the sergeant who was in charge if he minded if I took a walk through the neighborhood in one last effort to find him. The sergeant agreed, just to humor me. The search would have to be conducted without my portable radio because the battery had run down.

"As I had done on other occasions, I tried to put myself in the place of the criminal and imagine which way I would flee to avoid capture. I walked around the north side of the residence and then east, down a steep grassy bank—then into the back yard of a house just northeast of the house where the driver was arrested. There was a small open woodshed in the yard. Inside the woodshed was a garbage can turned upside-down. Sticking out of the bottom of the garbage can was a trace of blue jeans and a pair of black shoes. A black, bushy Afro wig, a jeans vest, and a pair of sunglasses were on the floor in the corner of the shed.

"I was so happy that I almost jumped out of my boots, but I realized that Curtis might be crouched in the garbage can with a gun pointed right at me. I took cover, fully expecting gunfire from the garbage can after the first words out of my mouth. I cocked my service revolver *(a rare practice—a hair-trigger condition is created)* and pointed it at the middle of the can and said; 'I want to see two empty hands come out from under that garbage can, or I'm going to blow the can full of holes.' Sure enough, the hands came out empty; and Curtis carefully lifted the can over his head and placed himself face down on the floor. Before I had a chance to read him his rights, he was pleading that his accomplice had forced him to do the robbery.

"Curtis had consumed a considerable amount of alcoholic beverage, and it was a practice at that time to videotape suspects who had consumed alcohol, when they were involved in serious crimes. The video taping was done in order to show the degree of intoxication at the time of arrest. This is one tape that I wish I could have saved for my own entertainment. Curtis was directed to stand in front of the camera, and Miranda Warnings were read to him. When asked if he understood his rights he said he did, and stated, ' —and furthermore, you violated my mo-fuckin' rights.' He told me that I had no business coming into that "mo-fuckin'" shed and looking under that garbage can.

"I said, 'If you are so innocent, why were you hiding under that garbage can?'

"Curtis responded, 'Man! It's none of your mo-fuckin' business what I was doing under that garbage can. For all you know, I live there.' The judge and the entire jury could not hold back laughter as they watched Curtis perform on the video.

"I did not have to go to trial on the driver of the Thunderbird, and I don't know what kind of sentence he received for his part in the robbery. Curtis had a terrible criminal history prior to meeting me. In 1966, a month after he turned eighteen, Curtis received a zero-to-ten-year sentence for auto theft. He was sent to the Shelton Reformatory. To earn that kind of sentence for auto theft, there had to have been some other serious considerations. Then, in 1972, Curtis was arrested and convicted for robbery and assault. He received a fifteen-year sentence for the robbery and 10 years for the assault. Notice that it wasn't enough for Curtis to rob someone, he had to hurt them also. In 1975, Curtis escaped from the Washington State Reformatory. For his escape, he received ten years that was suspended with one year probation after release from the reformatory. He was paroled to Seattle, April 1, 1977. That was certainly an "April fool" on Seattle. I arrested Curtis in October of that year.

"Curtis was not only found guilty of the robbery that I arrested him for — the King County Deputy Prosecutor filed for a second trial in an attempt to convict Curtis under the old "Habitual Criminal Act." That was a law similar to the current "Three Strike" law. Curtis was convicted and received the prescribed life sentence. It was my understanding that the sentence was supposed to be life without parole. I was wrong.

"Much to my surprise, Curtis was arrested for DUI and a probation violation in March 1988. He beat the DUI charge, and no action was taken on the probation violation. In June of that same year he was arrested for auto theft but was not charged. The reason he wasn't charged was probably because the prosecutors took the cheap way out, and they were satisfied that Curtis was being sent back to the reformatory for violating parole on the life sentence he received from my arrest.

"In November 1992, Curtis was arrested for robbery again and subsequently convicted and sentenced to 53 months in prison. In March 1996, Curtis was arrested for possession of stolen property. In June 1996, there was yet another arrest for Robbery and Malicious Mischief. In 1997, there was a warrant for the arrest of Curtis. Guess what the nature of the charge on the warrant was? You guessed it—robbery!

"The offenses committed by Curtis that have resulted in his arrest are the only criminal acts that he is known to have committed. Only the very naive would think that Curtis is just unlucky and is arrested almost every time he decides to commit a crime. The average citizen would realize that Curtis has probably committed anywhere from ten to a hundred or more crimes for every time he has been arrested. The question that continues to haunt me is, whatever happened to the life sentence for the habitual offender conviction back in 1977?"

Raylon Isn't With Us Any More. One of the most vicious criminals that Howard would face during his entire career was Raylon Raye. Fortunately, this meeting would occur on a day when Howard's reflexes and survival instincts were sharp. Near-death experience number six is described in the lucky cop's own words:

"Though homicide detectives in Seattle suspected that Raylon Raye was a "hit man" for a drug ring, few street cops were aware of his vicious criminal history. He was believed to have murdered people in Washington State and Canada. It was a case of strong suspicion, but there was not enough evidence to charge him with the crimes. I was having a lunch break with a couple of officers in South Seattle when a robbery *(with shots fired)* in the north end of town was broadcast over all police frequencies. The description was that of a black male who had robbed a wine truck driver at a grocery store and fired a shot in the commission of the robbery.

"An alert citizen heard the police broadcast on his scanner radio. He looked out of his living room window toward the grocery store and saw Raylon run across an open field and enter a taxicab. The witness noted the number of the taxi and phoned 911. Police radio announced what the witness had observed, and that the taxi was heading toward the South End. The officers who were with me jumped up and ran out the door. I yelled at them to sit tight and wait for the bandit to come and join us for lunch. I finished my lunch and paid my bill, while continuing to receive information about the cab. The police radio operator was in contact with the cab's dispatcher, and the cab driver would occasionally give his location. The dispatcher was pretending to have another fare waiting for that driver. When police units would arrive at locations where the cab driver had indicated he was due to arrive, witnesses would tell officers that the cab had been there and left. This raised suspicions that the cab driver might have been assisting the robber to escape.

"From the locations that the taxi driver was providing to the operator, it was evident that he was being evasive. The only way to find that cab was to anticipate the direction of travel and jump ahead of the locations he was providing.

"I turned my police motorcycle around, and within a few minutes the taxicab was in view. It is difficult to describe the feelings of exhilaration and fear that occurred simultaneously. The cabdriver had given so many locations that police units were spread out and the closest backup unit was about a mile away. The police motorcycle was no sooner positioned behind the cab than the driver panicked and stopped suddenly in the middle of a side street. There was not enough distance between the motorcycle and the cab for safety. A police motorcycle doesn't provide much cover in a gun battle. In such a position, one can only hope that the robber is a bad shot. Realizing that I was in extreme danger and maybe about to die, I experienced going into a kind of "automatic pilot" mode, a response that had happened to me during other stressful situations. Everything seemed to occur in slow motion, and it was as if I were watching this entire event unfold from outside my body. That big old Harley Davidson motorcycle stopped on a dime, and I was off the cycle with my gun in my left hand, holding the bike up with my right hand before putting the kickstand down. To this day, I do not remember drawing the gun from my holster. For some strange reason, I was attempting to put the kickstand down with my right heel *(a difficult thing to do)*, while pointing my gun at the door of the cab. Don't ask me why I didn't just let the motorcycle drop.

"Raylon bailed out of the left rear door of the cab, and I screamed, 'Run and I'll blow your fucking head off.' The profanity was another reflex resulting from my "dissociative response" *(discussed in detail in Chapter Three)* to this fearful circumstance. The use of strong language and my eyes being as big as saucers must have caused Raylon to believe that I was scared and crazy enough to shoot him, because he put his hands up and turned back toward the cab.

"Realizing that backup was quite a distance away, I had to take control of the situation before Raylon changed his mind about sticking around. I told him to put his hands on the roof of the cab. Keeping Raylon between me and the cab driver, who could have been an accomplice, I inched my way forward. There was also a woman passenger in the back seat. I took Raylon by the neck and backed away from the cab. He struggled and argued his innocence in an attempt to distract me, as the female slid out of the other side of the cab and began to walk away with a coat over her arm. I yelled to her that I would shoot if she

81

didn't return to the cab, but she continued walking. Obviously, I would not shoot the woman in the back. She entered an insurance office.

"Backup units arrived and found the woman accomplice in the insurance office. They discovered that she had hidden the gun, wallet, and money under a chair in the office. The Colt 38-caliber semiautomatic pistol was cocked with a round in the chamber, ready to fire at me if I hadn't kept Raylon in front of me. The gun had been under her coat and pointed at me as I used Raylon for a shield to back away from the cab. She had been given instructions to shoot me as I approached Raylon at the cab. I was lucky.

"It was especially exciting to learn of how notorious Raylon was. The gun he had used in this robbery had been taken from the owner of a Chinese restaurant, which Raylon had robbed the night before. Raylon was convicted of the wine-truck robbery; but he was not charged for the Chinese restaurant robbery because witnesses were unable to identify him in a lineup. He served about eighteen months in prison and then was released on parole.

"There was no spectacular police work involved in this arrest. It was only a matter of a cop anticipating the direction of travel of the criminal, and the cop allowing the criminal to stumble into him.

"No one was aware that Raylon had been released from prison. Robberies and rapes of women began occurring in parking garages in the downtown area. After a couple of months of a near epidemic of these crimes against women, a night shift unit spotted a stolen car that was taken from one of the rape victims. They began chasing the stolen car at high speeds through the downtown area. The stolen vehicle eventually crashed into a tree in Denny Park, and guess who was killed? Yes, it was Raylon. The parking garage rapes stopped. Poor Raylon! What a sad ending to this story. He was so young, and just getting started on his criminal career—cut down in the prime of his life."

There was no doubt in Howard's mind that Raylon's girlfriend would have killed him if he had not used Raylon for a shield. He recalled that the woman's coat was over her right hand as she was seated in the back of the cab. If there had not been a plan to shoot Howard, the gun would have been stuffed under the back seat.

A Smart, But Very Unlucky, Bank Robber. After his capture, William *(last name withheld out of respect for his mother)* was found to be responsible for about thirty bank robberies up and down the West Coast. The FBI had been frustrated in their attempts to find him. They had many bank photos of him, but they could not identify him. William was a former Los Angeles cop. He might have been fired because of alcohol abuse. He later became a probation officer for one of the Washington State penitentiaries and didn't make it there either. William's background had equipped him with the knowledge to formulate a profitable plan to extract money from banks and not get caught. He would catch a plane out of Los Angeles to a major city on the West Coast, using a false name. Rather than using a rental car or taxicab, William would use public transportation to get to the downtown area. He would pick any bank in a busy area and hand the teller a note that would terrify almost anyone. The note would indicate that he had a gun, he wanted all the money in the drawer; and if they sounded an alarm, he would blow them away. This man was 6 feet 6 inches tall and heavily built, so he didn't even have to hand someone a note like that to strike fear in their heart.

William always got the money he asked for, and then he would wait at a bus stop about forty-five minutes after the robbery. He would kill time in a department store, and after the initial search of the area by police, he would make his way to a bus stop eight to ten blocks from the bank. If a police unit approached the bus stop, he would just step back into the doorway of a business. Then he would take a bus back to the airport and leave town. William met his downfall when he came to Seattle on one of Howard's lucky days. In February 1980, Howard was part of a motorcycle escort for a small parade through downtown Seattle, when a bank robbery occurred just a few blocks from them. The description given was: white male; 35 to 40 years of age; 6 feet 6 inches tall; over 200 pounds, and sporting a beer belly—wearing red and white plaid shirt over a brown and white shirt, brown trousers, plaid fishing cap, with thick prescription eye glasses.

Most officers are aware that even the dumbest of criminals change their appearance after leaving the scene of a crime. One could anticipate that a man wearing those outrageous clothes would not be wearing those same items for very long after the robbery. Even eleven-year-old purse-snatchers change their appearance after their dirty deed. When looking for criminals described by witnesses, cops need to concentrate on physical appearance, and on items that are unlikely to change. In this particular case, distinguishing items such as the prescription glasses, the beer belly, short sandy hair, tall, and heavy build would be difficult to hide. Any white male downtown who was about 35 to 40-years-old, showing similar characteristics, would have been considered a possible suspect; even if he were dressed in a minister's robe.

Howard's sergeant saw that he wanted to leave the escort and catch the robber, and the sergeant ordered him to stay with the parade. Although heartsick, he followed orders. After completing the escort, Howard asked his partner to accompany him in searching the area for the bank robber. They searched for about twenty minutes, and their enthusiasm was wearing down. It was agreed that searching further was futile and that it was time to head for the coffee break that had already been delayed. Although Howard's conscious mind was thinking about coffee, his subconscious mind caused him to remain aware of persons in the crowd on the sidewalks. Nearing the coffee shop, they made a right turn from Cherry Street to Second Avenue. A large man quickly stepped back into the crowd of people at a bus stop. He had been standing at a location where he could observe the approach of a police unit for about three-quarters of a mile; but the officer's right turn surprised him, and he was slow in reacting. The man had a beer belly and thick glasses, and he was carrying a paper bag. The large man was not wearing a plaid shirt or a plaid fishing cap; but as previously mentioned, a cop wouldn't expect that. Howard stopped his motorcycle as quickly as possible and started pushing it back to the curb. His partner *(Jerry Hofstee)* was surprised at Howard's sudden stop, but he reacted quickly and followed.

A woman who had been standing next to the man was asked if she had seen where he had gone. She shrugged her shoulders as if she didn't even know a man had been standing next to her. Howard ran into the building that the man had been standing in front of and asked a person on the mezzanine stair landing if a large man had come up the stairs past him. The person hesitated as if he were wondering if he should help the cops or not. After yelling, "Well, did you or didn't you?" the man nodded and pointed up the stairway. Howard ran up to the second floor, while Jerry guarded the main floor level. While Howard was searching the second floor, William had taken the elevator to the basement to attempt his escape. He found that the basement fire exits were improperly chained shut. William decided to make it up the stairway to the lobby, and that is where he ran into Jerry. Howard was called by radio to return to the lobby to see if the man Jerry had detained was the same person who had been standing at the bus stop. He was the same guy. There was plenty of "reasonable suspicion" to protect themselves and check the man and his paper bag for weapons. Inside the bag was a lot of money and a robbery note.

William had never left a clue for the FBI in any of his many bank robberies, except for several clear photographs of William robbing banks in Sacramento, San Francisco, Portland, Salem, and Seattle. The FBI was grateful, and they mailed a commendation letter to Howard's chief. The commendation was a surprise because there was no extraordinary law enforcement performance in this incident. Being able to remain awake while on duty, and possessing a strong desire to catch the bad guy, should be an expectation for all cops. William was the epitome of a smart criminal with a good plan, who was captured because of a stroke of bad luck and an alert cop who cared.

"Suspect Shot After Wild Cross-Town Chase," was the headline in a major Seattle newspaper in 1980; and wild it was.

The only reason that the officers involved were not penalized is because no one except the suspect was injured. The trend to prevent officers from participating in high-speed vehicle pursuits continues to intensify. Many jurisdictions are leaning toward "no chase under any circumstance" policies.

In defense of cops who overreact when caught up in pursuits of criminals, there are studies of such situations that show a phenomenon sometimes referred to as "End of Pursuit Syndrome." The theory is that there is a tendency for cops to have difficulty breaking off from a pursuit and difficulty in resisting the use of unnecessary force after a stressful capture. This is an apparent explanation *(not an excuse)* for why cops ignore policies and exhibit poor judgement. It is tough for cops to back off once they have focused on apprehending a running or fighting subject. The public has had the opportunity to observe the effects of the "Pursuit Syndrome" on television now that video cameras are being installed in the grills of police cars. The high-tech camera equipment now in news helicopters offers a bird's-eye view of shocking overreactions by cops. Because of this "heat-of-the-chase" response, it is unrealistic to expect that an involved cop will make a proper decision to terminate a high-speed pursuit 100 percent of the time. That is why the burden of calling off a pursuit has been extended to partners and supervisors when the danger of the chase outweighs the threat to public safety posed by the escape of the suspect.

The villain in this story was a down-on-his-luck family man who decided that crime does pay *(as it most certainly does)*. The poor sap took the family gun and robbed a bank in the Ballard area. A witness saw him get into his van and phoned a description of the van to 911. An alert North Precinct cop saw the van, and the chase was on. Howard was in the downtown area on a police motorcycle as the chase approached his location. His heart sank as he mentally reviewed the rules concerning the pursuit of vehicles. Only two police cars were allowed to participate in a car chase. Police motorcycles could only be involved until a four-wheel vehicle took over. There was a loophole that allows other police units to get involved. Other units could parallel the car chase, but only by driving under normal patrol conditions—no emergency lights and no sirens. This was a difficult rule to follow for an officer who wanted to get into the act. As the fleeing van entered the heavy traffic of the downtown shopping area, Howard could hear the chasing units very near, and he began to parallel the locations that officers were screaming into their radio microphones. The van bounced off moving and parked cars, going the wrong way on one-way streets, and using the sidewalks when necessary. It was obvious that the driver of the van was trying to frighten the officers into abandoning the chase.

A newspaper interviewed various pedestrian witnesses, and the next day it published the following quotes: "The guy at the wheel looked so calm he could have been on a Sunday drive"— "He was doing about 35, swerving between buses and into the wrong lane, paying no attention to traffic lights, the right rear tire flapping and wobbling on the rim"— "Maybe his wife is having a baby and they're escorting him"— "Boy, is HE going to get a ticket!"

Howard valiantly attempted to obey department rules, and he only fudged a couple of times. He had to slip through some intersections against red lights in order to stay close to the chase. The van headed for the southbound entrance of Interstate 5, as it careened off the side of three more cars. Howard entered the freeway about six blocks in back of the chase and found that he was able to gain on the van easily in the heavy freeway traffic. The van had difficulty getting around the traffic as the robber frantically swerved from lane to lane. He finally got a good look at the van as the distance between them narrowed. It looked as if it had been involved in a demolition derby. The van left the freeway in the south end of Seattle, with two police cars close behind. South Precinct patrol units were closing in fast. As the van approached a red traffic signal at a major arterial, Howard was only two blocks behind. He had to dodge parts that were falling off the van. The cross traffic was heavy, and he held his breath as the van slipped between the moving cars on the cross street. As the van attempted a fast left turn to a narrow side street, it was met head-on by an oncoming station wagon. The robber's van was trapped after crashing into the station wagon.

Three or four patrol cars came to a screeching halt. When Howard arrived, the roadway was totally blocked. The robber got out and started running away on the sidewalk. Howard had to go over the curb to get by the blockade of police cars, and was quickly beside the running robber as he was nearing an alley. The robber started angling toward the alley.

Howard thought of riding up beside the man in the alley and bulldogging him to the ground, as the rodeo riders do. Another idea was just to run him over with the motorcycle. His wild imaginings were suddenly cut short as an officer yelled, "Stop or I'll shoot!" Just as Howard was about to cross the sidewalk area, only about three or four feet behind the robber, a shot rang out. Fear gripped his entire being. One of the last ways that he wanted to end his life was to get in the way of a bullet from another cop's gun. He jerked the motorcycle to a stop and yelled, "Don't shoot!" The robber took about two more running steps and dropped to the ground like a wounded deer. Howard was on top of him a second after he hit the ground. The robber was screaming in pain. Howard jerked his hands behind him and quickly handcuffed him as the captive moaned and groaned. That sounds cold hearted, but unrestrained, the robber was still capable of shooting the officers. Blood was streaming from his side. Howard pulled the robber's shirt up and saw a gaping hole where a bullet had entered his lower back. The bullet had exited at the side of his abdominal area, leaving a bloody mess. Money was sticking out of his belt. Howard reached into his waistband and pulled out a large wad of blood-soaked money. To everyone's astonishment, Howard took his Miranda Rights card out of his shirt pocket and read the warnings to the wounded man as he writhed in pain on the ground. Once again, Howard's actions appeared insensitive; but he didn't want some attorney trying to use the fact that the suspect wasn't given his rights to assist in his defense.

The Chief of Police was so concerned about the wild antics that he showed up while Howard was still on the ground with the suspect. The Chief had been understandably worried; but he offered no criticism because of the seriousness of the crime and, more importantly, because no innocent persons were hurt.

A Good Case For Never Talking To Strangers. Gale is a sex offender who should never again be free to victimize innocent young women. The justice system finally caught up with Gale when he was sentenced to twenty years in prison in 1981. He was incarcerated in the Washington State Correction Center in Shelton, with no chance of release until 2001. The justice system had failed miserably during the early years of this deviate's criminal history. One can only hope he is not allowed to walk the streets ever again. He could be held beyond the year 2001 if Washington's civil commitment law, which requires further detention for sex offenders who are likely to re-offend, will apply in his case. In 1974, Gale was charged with Sodomy and First-Degree Robbery. He was convicted of the Sodomy charge in early 1975, and the Robbery charge was dismissed. The sentence was twenty years, but he got off with ten years of supervision. In March 1977, Gale was committed to the Shelton Reformatory for a charge of Indecent Liberties. Someone must have thought that Gale was a pretty good risk, because on February 2, 1981, he was on work release when, by "accident," he made Howard's acquaintance. *(Car accident, that is)*.

At 5 p.m. Friday afternoon, on that fateful day in February, a pretty fifteen-year-old girl was walking home from an after-school activity near Northgate, in Seattle. Gale parked his car at the curb and was standing on the sidewalk as the girl *(call her Jane Doe)* approached. He asked Jane if she could direct him to a bus station. What she should have done was to keep her distance from the stranger, but most teenagers think they can handle any situation. She approached Gale, and thinking that he had asked about a bus stop, she turned and pointed up the block. He took that opportunity to grab Jane around the neck and place a knife to her neck as he dragged her to his car. Gale told her, "If you scream or say anything, I will slice your throat open." He forced her to lie face down across the front seat while he tied her hands behind her back with some cloth. He crawled over the top of her to reach the driver's seat and threatened her again, "Stay down and don't move or I'll cut your throat." He placed the point of the sharp object against her throat again and said, "I'll cut the vein in your throat and you'll bleed to death."

Gale drove around aimlessly while terrorizing his victim by asking, "Have you ever been raped before?" When Jane told him she hadn't, he replied, "Then this is going to be your first time." He asked her over and over again what her name was and how old she was. This went on for about fifteen minutes before Gale drove into the side of another car at a residential intersection. The other car was knocked into a yard on the corner. The force of the accident caused Gale to lose his thick glasses, and he became preoccupied with trying to locate them. He told Jane, "Keep your mouth shut. If you say anything, I will find you, and you will never go home again because I will kill you!" He untied Jane's hands so that the other driver would not be suspicious. The other driver walked to Gale's car and asked if they were all right. Gale said he was okay, and Jane said, "Yeah." Gale began looking on the floorboard for his glasses, and Jane took that opportunity to mouth the words, "Help me—RAPE—help me!" The man nodded to her that he understood, and he stayed beside the car.

Howard was in the area on a motorcycle and overheard police radio dispatch a patrol car to a serious accident on a side street. Although he was not assigned to the call, Howard rushed to the scene to check for injuries. The man beside Gale's car hurried over to the motorcycle officer and said, "Be careful with that guy—Something is wrong in that car—The girl whispered that she was going to be raped!" That got Howard's attention. The patrol officer arrived, and Gale was asked to step out of his car several times; but he continued whispering to Jane. Gale was ordered out of the car in a very stern manner. He had to be literally dragged from the driver's seat. As he exited the car, he continued to stare and whisper at the terrified girl. Gale took a seat in the patrol car so that the officer could get information to investigate the accident. Howard questioned Jane about her circumstances. The conversation was as follows:

"Is anything wrong?"

"I think my toe is broken."

"Isn't there something else wrong?"

"No, I'm afraid."

"What are you afraid of?"

"I can't say—he said he would find me."

"If he has threatened you, he won't be in any position to find you, because he will be in our custody. If you don't tell me what he has done wrong, we will have to let him go today."

(Crying) "He told me that he would find me and kill me if I tell the police what he had done."

"If he threatened or harmed you in any way, he will be going to jail. And we will have to release him after we investigate this accident if you don't tell us what he has done."

Jane broke down and told Howard the frightful story of her abduction. He knew that if she were a reluctant witness, or if her parents were uncooperative, the prosecutor would end up with a very weak case. A veteran officer, Don Mills, was assigned to take Jane home, with instructions to brief the parents on the matter and obtain a written statement from Jane. Fortunately, with the support of her parents, Jane turned out to be a very strong witness, and the officer obtained an incriminating written statement from her that would make any defense attorney shudder. Officer Mills' compassion and experience in dealing with victims played a large part in the success of the interview.

Gale was arrested for Assault, Abduction, and Narcotics. A full bag of suspected marijuana, illegal mushrooms, and narcotic pills was found before impounding Gale's car. At the precinct, Gale said that he was going to his mother's house and saw Jane hitchhiking, so he decided to help her out. When asked where he was taking her, he responded that he didn't know, but he was just going to drop her off wherever she told him to. Someone at the precinct recognized that Gale was the infamous "Greenlake Rapist" from the 1970s. It was astounding that he would be out on work release. While in the temporary holding cell at the North Precinct, Gale pounded on the door and yelled, "I need to take a piss." Normally, one officer would accompany a prisoner to the rest room as long as the prisoner had not exhibited hostility; but Gale seemed so desperate that another officer was asked to assist. Howard's suspicion proved correct, as

Gale really didn't have to go. He stood for a while at the urinal and faked it. While walking to and from the restroom, Gale was looking in every direction for an escape route. He wanted to run.

After necessary paperwork was completed, two young officers were assigned to transport Gale to the King County Jail. Howard was concerned that Gale would continue to look for an opportunity to escape. Gale had nothing to lose, so a conference was held in the holding cell with the two transporting officers and Gale. The young officers were briefed on Gale's criminal history and told that he was the Greenlake Rapist, out on a work release program when he grabbed the little girl. Howard explained exactly what Gale had done in the past and what he had threatened to do on that day. He said, "This is my prisoner, and considering his history and what he has done today, if he were about to escape from custody, I would not hesitate to blow his *(expletive deleted)* head off." Howard continued, "Since you are transporting my prisoner, I would expect you to take the same action—did I make that clear enough?" He asked Gale if he understood, and Gale just gave him an unhappy look. This was such a strong case that Gale was forced to plead guilty to First Degree Kidnapping to avoid other charges. As mentioned earlier, he was given a twenty-year sentence. What worries everyone involved with Gale is what he will do to his next victim when he is released. Howard is convinced that Gale will not leave his next victim(s) alive to testify against him.

There was absolutely no special talent involved in this memorable capture of a major criminal. The arrest was merely the result of responding to an accident call. There was no apparent danger to the officers during the capture of one of the most vicious criminals an officer could lay hands on during a career; but Howard wonders how much hatred Gale has harbored while serving his long prison sentence. The danger may be yet to come.

King Of Crooks Beats The System. A little crook, nicknamed "Mac," came to Seattle from New England to make his mark in the world of crime. There is no doubt that his goal was to be the "king pin" of hoodlums in Seattle. This one-man crime wave, and his ability to avoid prosecution, leaves one mystified. Howard tells it this way:

"My acquaintance with Mac began when I received a police radio call of a jewelry store robbery in the downtown area. The robber was seen running to a tattoo parlor two blocks from the jewelry store. I arrived at the tattoo parlor within minutes of the robbery, and the owner of the parlor said the man I described to him had used his phone to call a cab. Working through the taxi company dispatcher, our police radio operator was able to get the number of the cab that had transported the robber. The radio operator asked the cab to meet me at a downtown location. The driver was able to give me the address of the old fleabag hotel where he had dropped the robber. Once at the hotel, we found an open door on the second floor; and we could plainly see evidence from the jewelry store robbery within the room. Other residents revealed that several persons used that room to crash, and one of those persons was Mac.

"Mac was taken into custody when he exited another room on the second floor and was taken to headquarters for questioning. I had a chance to talk with Mac about the robbery, and, of course, he said he was an innocent victim of circumstance. He said another person who crashed in that room must have committed the robbery. After our detectives interviewed Mac, he was released, pending further investigation.

"Mac had just exited the headquarters precinct when I happened to pass the bulletin board containing wanted persons. I noticed a picture of an armed robbery of a downtown hotel which had been taken by a hidden camera. The man holding a gun on the desk clerk was none other than Mac himself. I showed the picture to the robbery detectives right away. They wanted to believe that it might not be Mac in the picture, but there was no doubt that it was. The detectives were just embarrassed because a lowly motorcycle officer had connected Mac to the wanted poster. The detectives indicated that they would like to talk to Mac once again.

"In the next week or two, we had a rash of robberies—

another hotel, a porno movie, a restaurant, and another jewelry store. The description of at least one of the suspects in each robbery always matched our buddy Mac. About two weeks after my original meeting with Mac, my partner *(Jerry Hofstee)* and I were assigned to work a late shift for DUI emphasis during the holidays. Jerry was standing by, as I had a potential drunk driver stopped on a busy 40-mph arterial. While I was in the street talking to the stopped driver, a passing car swerved and nearly struck my police motorcycle and me. Jerry then pursued the erratic driver. I finished issuing a speeding ticket to the driver I had stopped *(who had turned out to be sober)*, and I hurried to catch up with my partner. I found him about one mile north of my original stop. He was on a side street, conducting physical tests on the driver who had nearly struck me. There were two plain-clothes Vice Unit detectives backing him up as he was showing the very large drunk driver how he wanted him to walk "heel-to-toe" in a straight line. The vice officers had witnessed the unusual driving of the DUI and had also witnessed that he had almost struck me while I was in the street.

"I noticed that the guy Jerry was testing was one mean-looking dude. He was about 6 feet 5 inches tall and weighed 260 pounds. He made Jerry look like a midget at 5 feet 10 inches. I was glad the vice detectives had been there to back Jerry, not only because of the size of the driver, but also because there were three other seedy-looking characters seated in the car. The guy in the front passenger seat looked familiar. I moved in for a closer look and saw that he was my old robber friend Mac. I hurried back to the vice car and asked the detectives to assist me in shaking down the car for weapons *(a procedure judged not to be a violation of Fourth Amendment rights under these circumstances)*. We approached carefully, shined flashlights into the car, and told the occupants not to move their hands. I could see two rifles under the feet of the two men in the back seat. We took the three men out of the car, patting them down for weapons. We then confiscated the two rifles from the rear car floor. I greeted Mac and read him his Miranda rights.

"I had our radio operator call the robbery office to find out if the detectives still wanted to talk to Mac about the hotel robbery. The message I received was that the detectives were eagerly awaiting the return of my little robber friend. It appeared that Mac was located just in time, because he had airline tickets to his hometown in his pocket for the following day. My partner arrested the huge driver for DUI and Reckless Driving.

"I interviewed the big guy when we got back to headquarters. Our conversation went something like this:

"'What were you and Mac up to tonight?'

"'I was driving Mac to a liquor store at 45th and Stone.'

"'Was Mac going to the store to rob it?'

"'No—He wanted to buy some booze.'

"'You guys hang around the downtown area. Why are you going to a liquor store in the north end of town?'

"'That's the only liquor store I know how to get to.'

"'Didn't you think it was strange that Mac was taking two rifles to the liquor store with him?'

"'Look, man, when Mac tells you to drive him somewhere, you don't ask him any questions – you just drive him there!'

"This last statement, reflecting the large man's fear of and respect for such a shrimp, really struck me funny. That little jerk must really have had a good "tough act" to get that much respect from an animal of a guy who outweighed him by a hundred pounds or more and towered over him by almost a foot.

"The next day, our detectives placed Mac in a lineup that was viewed by victims of robberies from porno theaters, jewelry stores, hotels, and liquor stores. We knew that Mac was the actual armed robber, not only from photographs taken by security cameras, but also from information I was able to pry out of the big DUI driver. The big guy told me that Mac had been bragging about the porno and restaurant holdups. Out of all of the witnesses and victims viewing the lineup, not one could pick Mac out of the group and identify him as the robber.

"This usually means that, for lack of enough other independent evidence, Mac would have to be released and not charged for the robberies we knew he committed. You cannot blame the witnesses for not being able to pick Mac out of a crowd at the lineup. He had changed his hairstyle, and he was growing a mustache. Another factor is that it is not easy to pay much attention to the features of an individual when you are staring down the barrel of a large caliber pistol. Mac committed all of those robberies and got away clean. He was laughing at our justice system, but we had an ace in the hole *(we thought)*. While I was checking Mac for weapons on the night we took him in, I found that he had a trick belt buckle that had an illegal fold-out knife. We charged Mac with the misdemeanor, "Carrying an Illegal Dangerous Knife." About a month later, I was surprised to see that Mac showed up in Seattle Municipal Court for his trial. I thought he would have left town with the trial coming up; but he showed, represented by a public defender.

"Everything was going fine for our side until his lawyer pulled the following ingenious trick:

LAWYER: "Officer, how long before this arrest had you known my client by his name?"

ME: "About a week or two."

LAWYER: "During that time, isn't it true you and the detectives believed that there was probable cause to arrest my client for robbery?"

ME: "Yes"

LAWYER: "Was there anything to prevent you or the detectives from attempting to obtain a warrant for the arrest of my client?"

ME: "No."

"The following is the attorney's argument to the judge for dismissal of the case against his client:

"'Your honor, I move to dismiss the charge of Carrying a Dangerous Knife which is being brought against my client. The search of my client was the product of an illegal warrantless arrest. The officer thought there was probable cause to arrest my client for a full week; and neither he nor the detectives took time to apply for an arrest warrant. Since the arrest was improper, the ensuing search was also improper; and the charge should be dismissed.'

"A good prosecuting attorney could have countered the public defender's argument easily, by arguing that the search for weapons on the person of a passenger in a car with two rifles on the rear floor was a lawful search, but the prosecutor was caught speechless by the innovative move. That public defender later became one of the most competent judges I have encountered on the Seattle Municipal Court Bench.

"The Judge in Mac's case agreed with the public defender's argument. Due to lack of a challenge from the prosecuting attorney, Mac and his little entourage of goons left the court room grinning. I never did get the last laugh on that guy. I haven't heard from Mac in over ten years, but I'll bet that he is doing his act in the downtown area of some other city." *(End of motorcycle stories).*

For fifteen years, performing law enforcement duties while riding a motorcycle was the ultimate thrill. Howard told his associates that, for him, the felony arrests had the exhilarating effect of a mood-elevating drug. He said that if he didn't make a difficult and important arrest at least once every month, he would become depressed. Howard loved his job so much that he planned to remain a motorcycle officer until his retirement. Things change, and a nasty accident in his twelfth year on bikes initiated a change of attitude toward two-wheelers that eventually motivated him to transfer to the Patrol Division. A promotion to sergeant soon followed.

Photograph by Denis Law, 1973 (permission to republish granted).
Howard A. Monta overlooking scene of arrest of shoe store robber / escapee from Oregon.

CHAPTER 8

Big Motorcycle Accident

"Into each life some rain must fall." *(From the poem, "The Rainy Day," by Longfellow.)* If that is the case, it poured on Howard in October 1983, just one week after his forty-fifth birthday, and twelve years into his fifteen-year police motorcycle career.

When Howard was new to the Seattle Police Motorcycle Unit, he was told by veterans that, "While working the job of a motorcycle cop, it is not a question of *if* the officer will be involved in a serious traffic accident; it is a matter of *when* the accident(s) will occur, and how serious the injuries will be. One of Howard's favorite witticisms was, "We would write anyone else a Negligent Driving ticket for operating a motorcycle in the same manner that we operate our police motorcycles all day, every day—and they pay us for this!"

Reason would dictate that to catch fast and/or erratic drivers, a cop must operate his or her motorcycle in a faster and/or more erratic manner. Howard was involved in three relatively minor accidents prior to the "big one." Early in his first year on bikes, he was behind a City Light truck while completing a left turn to a major street. As they came out of the turn, people on the sidewalk caught Howard's attention. It was too late when he noticed the truck stop for oncoming traffic, waiting to make a left turn into a driveway. Howard locked his rear brakes and managed to slow his speed to about 10-mph before piling into the rear of the truck. Upon impact, he flew straight up in the air. A tight hold on the handlebars caused his arms to be nearly ripped from the shoulder sockets. He plummeted straight back down to the seat of the Harley Hog, which was still upright. Motorcycle and officer remained motionless for two seconds before both tipped over onto the pavement like a scene from a comedy show. Gordy Sackett, one of the legends in the motor-cycle unit, took Howard aside and told him, "Look, kid, you are going to have to remember — if they're good enough to stare at, they're worth going around the block and parking so you can ogle them safely."

Howard replied, "Gordy—that is not the case here." "That's what they all say," he shot back. If anyone knew all of the tricks of the trade when it came to the police motorcycle job, it would have been Gordy. He was in his fifties. He had wavy gray hair and the athletic build of a man of thirty. As would be expected after spending most of his life on motorcycles, Gordy's face had that "weathered" look. His skin resembled wrinkled and dried-out leather. Most alarming were his cold-as-steel eyes, which screamed out, "Don't mess with me!" Howard could not imagine anyone ever arguing with him about a ticket he issued. None-theless, Gordy had a sense of humor that could immediately override his appearance and set anyone at ease. He retired in his late fifties. Gordy drove a truck for a few years after retire-ment, but he passed away at much too young an age.

Another word of wisdom from Gordy that Howard always treasured was, "You always keep at least one eye on the road ahead. You can let the other eye wander if you are physically able to do that." Howard followed Gordy's advice religiously; but as hard as he tried, once in a while, imminent danger es-caped his view.

With each year that passed, Howard became a more defen-sive motorcycle rider. The warnings that he received from Gordy and other veterans were validated by accident after accident involving his friends. Many were devastating, but none were more heartbreaking than the loss of one of Howard's best friends, Jerry Wyant, on October 26, 1976. Jerry was a fun-loving guy, with a permanent ear-to-ear smile, and it was hard to imagine him writing a traffic ticket to anyone. You knew that if he wrote a traffic citation, it was really deserved. Everyone loved the guy, especially the women. He was short in stature for a motorcycle cop; but his good build, handsome face, thick and dark eyebrows, and dark wavy hair prompted women to fall all over him. He reminded one of the actor Robert Blake, who played the part of a motorcycle cop in the movie, *ElectraGlide In Blue.*

Jerry was patrolling on First Avenue South, in the industrial area of Seattle, on an overcast, dreary day. The investigation of his accident later revealed that Jerry was northbound in the left lane of First Avenue and was signaling to change one lane to his right. He had passed by a friend to his right who waved at him from the sidewalk. It would be characteristic of Jerry to go around the block to chat. Howard speculated that as Jerry was starting to change lanes he was checking his right mirror and glancing to the right rear to make sure no vehicles were overtaking him. Simultaneously, a large moving van pulled out from a stop sign on Dawson Street, attempting to cross four lanes of traffic on First Avenue. The truck driver did not see the approaching police motorcycle and continued into Jerry's path. The motorcycle struck the right front fender of the truck, causing Jerry to hurtle over the handlebars. The back of his helmet and neck struck the turn signal that was mounted on top of the truck fender. In the 1970s, motorcycle officers did not wear a full cover helmet. In Seattle they wore a three-quarter version that exposed the base of the skull, with only a leather cover over the ears. Jerry was severely injured, even though he had been traveling at only 25 to 30-mph.

Howard was four to five miles away, in Rainier Valley. When the accident involving an officer was broadcast over police radio, he lit his bike up and was the second officer to arrive at the scene. Jerry lay unconscious, as Fire Department Medics worked on him in the street. They slipped a flat board under him and carefully moved him to the aid car.

The hours Howard agonized in the Harborview Medical Center waiting room seemed like days. The anxiety level of waiting officers rose as an emergency-room doctor approached them. The doctor said, "Officer Wyant has suffered severe nerve damage in his neck, in addition to his head injury. He is still unconscious."

Howard asked, "Will he be ok?"

The doctor replied, "Even if by some miracle he regains consciousness, we have no way of knowing the extent of damage to his brain. A major nerve has been severed in his neck. He is now paralyzed from his neck down. If he lives, he will have to cope with that, and with serious brain damage." The news could not have been worse than that. Jerry passed away that day. His friends were spared the agony of seeing him paralyzed and brain-damaged.

Howard had great difficulty dealing with the death of his friend. Having been at the accident scene added to his grief. No one held any animosity toward the truck driver, who was devastated over his driving error. He was cited for "Failing to Yield The Right-of-Way From Stop Sign." It was a tragic accident, and everyone realized that he had not been driving in a negligent or reckless manner. Howard was certain that Jerry would have been able to avoid the truck if he had not been preoccupied by changing lanes.

The funeral was held on Broadway, near Seattle Central Community College. The entire motorcycle unit was assigned to ride escort for the vehicle procession to the cemetery in Lake City. As the funeral service was nearing conclusion, the escort officers lined their motorcycles along the street behind the college. Howard was seated on his bike, slumped over and sobbing. Some smart-ass, disheveled student was amused. The student walked up to the front of Howard's motorcycle and said, "What's goin' on, man?" in a marijuana-distorted tone.

Howard did not look up, but angrily replied, "Get this dumb son-of-a-bitch away from me before I beat the shit out of him." Officers on both sides of Howard escorted the laughing jerk away. Though Howard was known to be a non-violent person, this guy had picked the wrong time to pull his chain. The funeral procession was a long one, and Howard was in agony for the entire distance. There is no way he should have been allowed to perform that duty, but no one believed they dare stop him. He eventually came to terms with his friend's death, aided by the knowledge that Jerry died while doing what he loved to do.

Jerry Wyant's death had a significant effect on the intensity of Howard's vigilance while riding bikes. Even so, he was knocked down two more times before the "big one." One sunny day he was on a four-lane arterial street, passing a school bus on his right that was slowing on a slight curve. A driver hurried to pull out from a stop sign in front of the approaching bus, thinking that she could swing a right turn directly into the left lane to dodge out of the way of the bus. Obviously, she did not see the motorcycle passing the bus, and Howard had no idea that the car was going to appear directly in front of him. There was oncoming traffic, so Howard could not swerve left to avoid striking the left rear fender of the car. Fortunately, the bus driver anticipated what was happening, and was able to avoid running over both Howard and the car. His helmet and right shoulder struck the side of the car very hard. The helmet did its job, and injuries were minor.

On another occasion, Howard approached a car that was stopped to make a left turn. The left-turn signal was operating as the car waited for oncoming traffic to pass by. As the police motorcycle was about to pass on the right, the driver changed his mind and made an abrupt right turn. Howard locked his brakes and started to lay the motorcycle on its side, as he was trained to do. They collided before the bike was on the ground. The impact caused the bike to flip up and slam Howard against the side of the car. He remained upright, staring down into the face of the driver's mother. The only thing he could think of to say was, *Why are you making a right turn when you were signaling to turn left?* As it turned out, it was the mother who told the young driver to turn right, instead of left.

Not long after Jerry Wyant's death, another close friend, Officer Jerry Hofstee, was involved in a high-speed crash on Airport Way South *(a four-lane arterial in an industrial area of Seattle).* He and Howard were on their way to a sandwich shop, and Howard needed to stop at a bank for some lunch money. While Howard was at the drive-up window, a police motorcycle accident on Airport Way was broadcast on his radio. As soon as he heard the radio call, Howard knew who was involved. In a panic, he roared out of the bank lot. He later found out that a speeding Camaro had passed the bank lot, and Jerry couldn't resist the challenge. Traveling southbound on Airport Way, Jerry reached speeds in excess of 50-mph in the 30-mph zone, to overtake the fast-moving car. He was about to pass a large truck to his right. At the same time, a motorist was pulling out from a side street in front of the truck, turning left to travel northbound. Jerry had just flown by the truck as the turning car was pulling out. The truck driver later stated that he had to brake hard to avoid striking the emerging car himself. Jerry didn't have an opportunity to see the car he was about to hit until it entered his lane. His Harley Davidson Hog demolished the left front of the car. Instinctively, he had raised up from his seat before impact and was launched over the hood of the car. The force of the impact from the large bike turned the car ninety degrees, causing the right front wheel to roll and stop against Jerry's legs. When Howard arrived at the scene, his heart sank. The first thing he saw was a demolished Harley against a crumpled car, but no Officer Jerry Hofstee in sight. Howard was relieved to find him alive and not seriously hurt. He was on the pavement under the front of the car. It was a miracle he survived, suffering only a painful leg injury.

Jerry thought the accident was much more serious also. He said that when he looked to see what was causing all of the pressure against his legs, he could see that the tire was lodged against him. He also was shocked to see that his black uniform trousers ended at his knees. There was "nothing but red" below his knees. Jerry's immediate thought was that his lower legs had been severed; but he was relieved to find that what he had seen was his red long johns under the shredded legs of his uniform. After release from his hospital examination, Jerry received a call from a friend and veteran Accident Investigation Unit detective, Hal Fogus. Hal asked him if he was able to get the license number of the car that hit him. Hal told Jerry that the car drove off after medics loaded Jerry into the aid car, and no one had obtained the identity of the driver. He was devastated until Hal could no longer hold his laughter back. Sometimes that's what cops like to do to each other. They call it camaraderie.

A few months later, Jerry testified against the driver in Municipal court. While testifying in his own defense, the errant driver was asked to explain what he saw of the accident. He testified in broken English, "All I see is policeman with blue lights on, jump off motorcycle." The driver was convicted and paid a small fine for a minor traffic infraction. Jerry was riding his new Harley on a downtown street as he left the courthouse, when he met up with his favorite driver again. Out of nowhere, a car pulled in front of him and he had to lay the Harley on its side to avoid an accident. Jerry was amazed to see the familiar face of the guy who had nearly killed him on Airport Way. What a small world! He struggled to his feet and told the guy, "Get out of here!" *Why bother to write this idiot a ticket?* he thought to himself.

By his twelfth year on motorcycle duty, Howard was so defensive a driver, he would tell his fellow cops, "If anyone is going to hit me, they are going to have to try real hard!" This was the year that he found that one exceptional driver who not only hit him, but nearly killed him. On October 13, 1983, Howard was attempting to catch up with a driver who had failed to stop for a pedestrian in a crosswalk in the Ballard area. He had the emergency lights flashing and was operating the siren periodically to move cars to the right lane, so that he could pass. A driver in the left lane would not move over. They were doing the speed limit in a 30-mph zone; but Howard was having trouble catching up to the traffic violator, who was still several cars ahead.

As they approached a cross street, the stubborn guy ahead finally got the idea that a police motorcycle wanted to get past him. His brake lights went on, and it looked like he was starting to pull to the right. Oncoming traffic was pulling over and stopping for the emergency lights. Howard moved to the centerline and was starting to pass the car in front when it veered suddenly toward the left. The driver had panicked and thought it would be best to make a left turn to get out of the cop's way. The turn was started twenty-five feet before reaching the intersection. There was no time to react. The motorcycle struck the side of the car's left front fender, sending Howard airborne. He flew completely over the hood and struck the pavement, helmet and right shoulder first. Howard learned the account of the accident many months later. He was rendered unconscious, and had no memory of events leading up to the accident.

Howard awoke hours later in the Neurosurgery Unit of Harborview Medical Center. He had absolutely no memory for a few hours, not even a clue as to who he was. He had a foggy memory of teams of doctors and nurses walking through, sometimes asking confusing questions like, "Do you know your name—your birth date—what year it is—who is president?" Howard got the impression from the puzzled looks on their faces that he was not giving correct answers.

A familiar looking woman came in with a concerned expression on her face. She asked, "Howard, do you know who I am?"

He thought for a moment and answered, "You're Liz, my wife—Aren't you?"

She said, "Yes—Do you know how old you are?"

That was a very confusing question. With a baffled look on his face, he answered in a questioning tone, "Twenty?"

Her face dropped as though the world was about to end. She asked, "Don't you remember that we celebrated your forty-fifth birthday last week?"

A startled and anxious space cadet blurted, "You mean I'm forty-five years old? How old are you, then?"

Liz responded, "I'm forty-three."

"Oh, my God!" Howard shouted. He could relate to the fairytale, Rip VanWinkle, as he too felt he had slept away many years of his life.

Each day, bits and pieces of his memory began to return. Short-term memory remained nonexistent. Everything seemed like a foggy dream. Those teams of doctors and nurses continued to come and go; but he could never remember what they wanted, or what they were doing. Howard had to sleep with the hospital bed in an upright position because of broken ribs and a broken clavicle bone. To add to his misery, his right foot had been crushed when the crash bar on the motorcycle folded on impact. Sometime during the second day, Howard tipped his head back to look over his shoulder to the left. The room started turning end-over-end, until his field of vision was a big blur. There was a sensation of falling into a deep well, and he became sick to his stomach. Howard thought he was having some kind of seizure, or a stroke. He was sure he was dying. All he could do was to scream for help. It must have sounded like someone falling off a 10-story ledge, because people came running. In a minute or two *(that seemed like eternity)* the awful swirling subsided. Howard explained what had happened. A doctor told him that he probably had injured that portion of his inner ear which helps maintain equilibrium. He called the nightmare Howard had just experienced "positional vertigo." It did not take long to learn to avoid tipping his head back to the left. That severe reaction lasted for five months. The severity of the vertigo slowly subsided; however, it would remain in a milder degree for the rest of his life.

After a couple of days, Howard began to realize what had happened to him. Remaining propped up in the hospital bed all day and night bothered him; but when he attempted to lie flat, pain would shoot through his chest and right shoulder. Lying flat would also set off the vertigo. After three days in the Neurosurgery Unit, he heard talk of sending him home. "How am I going to exist if I leave here?" he worried, "Everything is so confusing, and I can't remember what has happened from moment to moment." Worry became his greatest misery—even more so than the excruciating pain and dizziness. He made up his mind that he would assemble that elusive group of doctors and nurses, and get some answers out of them. Whenever they were there he tried to talk to them, but they were always so busy. When they were starting to walk away, Howard would remember that he wanted to question them. He would put up his hand, saying, "Well, wait; I need to talk to you!" They would turn around and see a confused old cop with a blank stare on his face—then turn and walk away.

He finally collected his thoughts enough to keep the attention of a kind nurse. He told her, "I have some questions about things that have been worrying me, and I can't get the doctors to talk to me about them."

She responded, "Well, you tell me what is bothering you and I will ask the doctors about it."

Howard answered, "I am worried about leaving the hospital; I don't know how I will get by at home, because I can't do anything for myself. I won't even be able to sleep on my bed." The nurse assured him that he could rent a hospital bed for his home. She asked what else was bothering him. His facial expression went from interested to confused. "There were other things that I was worried about, but I can't remember what they were."

The nurse replied with a smile, "Could it be your lack of memory that worries you?" Howard's face lit up.

"That's it," he yelped, "I can't remember anything."

"I'll have the doctor explain what is happening with your memory. Don't worry, you will get it back." That gave Howard some peace of mind; however, he couldn't remember the other reasons he was afraid to go home, like, how was he going to shower and get around with his right leg in a cast and his right arm in a sling?

On the fourth day after the accident, Howard reluctantly went home to a hospital bed in his living room. He still did not have much of a clue as to what was going on. He was a terrible burden to his wife, but he didn't realize it. His actions and conversations must have been somewhat entertaining, because they were so bizarre. Short-term memory continued to be a problem. Long-term memory returned little by little; but he was never able to remember the accident, or much of anything else that happened within a couple days thereafter. Friends and relatives would come to visit for what seemed to be the sole purpose of testing, or maybe assisting, his memory. Jerry Hofstee brought an arrest report that Howard had written just an hour or two before the accident.

Early in their shift on the morning of the accident, Jerry, Michael T., and Howard had taken a coffee break on Aurora

Avenue, near the Woodland Park Zoo. Coming out of the coffee shop, Howard noticed an erratically driven car northbound on Aurora. He decided to take a look. The car turned out to be stolen. The fact that was most significant in jarring Howard's memory was that the auto thief was a woman. It was the only female auto thief whom he had personal experience with up until that time. It pleased Jerry to see Howard's face light up when a little piece of his memory returned.

It was a long three months in that hospital bed before Howard could lie in a horizontal position to sleep. The greatest problem, once he got back to the flat bed, was the vertigo. Every time his head would change position, he would awaken, feeling dizzy and nauseous. The trauma of the accident, combined with the inactivity of a guy who for all of his life had been hyperactive, caused Howard's mental health to deteriorate. His attorney told him that since his memory was so bad, he should keep a diary that described his recovery. Some selected diary pages follow, describing Howard's misery:

10-25-83 / Bad sleep—Lots of chest and shoulder pain. Avoided pain pills. I woke up 8 a.m. still exhausted. Tom Sutton took me to watch motorcycle training. I became light headed and dizzy when changing my position. Came home exhausted, but couldn't nap because of pain in chest and shoulder. Tried to go to sleep 8 p.m. while watching TV. Couldn't sleep. Took two codeine pain pills about 10 p.m. Went to sleep about 11 p.m. Discomfort woke me up about 3 a.m.— Restless sleep until 6:30 a.m. Out of pain pills.

11-01-83 / Chest now hurts front, side, and back. All of my chest muscles are sore, and right shoulder still sore. Woke up at 7 a.m.—went back to bed in living room about 11:30 a.m. to try to nap but laid there about 2 hours unable to sleep because of chest pain. Tried to read stories in National Geographic Magazine in afternoon, but I have trouble with concentration. I read parts of articles, and looked at pictures. My trouble with concentration and forgetfulness has been worrying me. Yesterday while talking on phone, I noticed that I stutter. I have never had a speech problem that I was aware of. I think I stutter at times now, because I forget what words I want to use. Noticed again today that I get emotional very easily. Got tears in my eyes reading an article about the Sonics basketball game in the newspaper. That's weird! I feel guilty looking at my poor dog— a two-year-old German Shepherd. We have had this dog about nine months and have been taking him for runs six mornings a week until my accident. Am so depressed that I can't even walk him to the park now. Also depressed because I miss my work and miss running around Greenlake three mornings per week. It seems like I might never be able to do that again. Don't feel suicidal, but sometimes I wish I wouldn't have survived this accident.

11-18-83 / Asked Dr Hatsukami if he would check my brain scan, because I was worried and didn't want to worry for two weeks until my next appointment to find out about my scan. Waited for about an hour for him to check it, and he told me I had no clots or bleeding, and my symptoms are normal for a serious head injury. He said I should get better. He told me that if I continued to have problems with depression and moods, that I could get medication to help. He said it is common to have temper problems.

12-01-83 / Needed two pain pills to get a night's sleep because of chest pain. I woke up very sore. Exercised, but couldn't do any sit-ups because of my chest pain. Went to Neurosurgery appointment at 2:30 p.m. The doctor said that my depression is normal for a severe concussion. Along with the paranoia and attitude and emotional problems I have been having, the doctor said that the dizzy spells that I have when I change position are called vertigo. He said that if it continues for another two weeks, I should return for another appointment — otherwise Neurosurgery clears me to go back to work on Dec. 23, if Orthopedics OKs my foot and collarbone.

12-29-83 / Neurosurgery appointment. Dr. Craven rechecked my last CT scan and found a gap between my brain and my forehead that might be fluid. I am scheduled for another CT scan next Wednesday, Jan 4. It will be taken face down to determine if it is fluid that is causing my problems. Now taking the drug, Meclizine, which is an antihistamine that makes me drowsy and sickly. Guess they think that will help get rid of the fluid. I took two pills today and feel zonked. Have an appointment for an ear specialist on Wednesday.

01-05-84/ (After returning to duty) 10:00 a.m. appointment with police dept. psychologist. Talked about depression and my lack of confidence about going back to work. Went to Neurosurgery at 1:30 p.m. A surgeon checked my latest brain scan and said there was a small amount of fluid in my forehead from the injury, but shouldn't cause a continuing problem. I asked if that caused my dull headache, and dull depression, and he said it was not the fluid, but the injury itself; he called it "Post" something. I asked if it would go away, and he said it may or may not. He released me for work with no restrictions, and told me to come back in two months.

01-06-84 / Woke up with dull headache—went to work at 10:30 a.m. Made my first traffic stop at about 12:35 p.m., and my headache began to throb, and was bad the rest of the day. My supervisor is having me work in a car for one-month trial before going back to the police motorcycle. I took lunch break at home at 2:30 p.m. and was sick to my stomach and had the throbbing headache. Didn't eat much. Toward the end of the shift I got a little lightheaded at times, but kept control. Remained nauseous the entire shift.

The diary notes do not fully describe the extent of Howard's problems. He left out things that embarrassed him, like barricading himself in his basement from his wife. He was convinced that she wanted to kill him while he slept. As time went by, the attitude of this once dedicated crime fighter deteriorated to the point where he began to think that he had been doing the wrong thing for all of those years—that he had been on the wrong side, and "oppressing the poor." He also had the notion that the administration and officers of the police department did not like him. There was a strong feeling that if he did not go back to work soon, his mental state would deteriorate to the point where he could never go back. He went to a psychologist outside the police department with his problems. The first thing he said to the psychologist was, "I know what's wrong with me, doctor."

The doctor asked, "What do you think is wrong?"

The answer was, "I'm paranoid— I've dealt with people like me."

"No, you are not paranoid," he responded.

"Well, if I'm not paranoid, what am I?" the bewildered cop asked.

The doctor answered, "You are suffering from Posttraumatic Stress Syndrome."

Howard questioned, "Isn't that the same thing as paranoia?"

"Well, I guess it is similar," he replied. Howard submitted to hypnosis therapy for his stress, and much to his surprise, it was amazingly helpful.

Howard was in no shape, mentally or physically, to return to work. His confidence level was below zero, but neither he nor the medical doctors realized how bad off he was. It was a challenge to Howard's ego to attempt a return to motorcycles, even though deep inside he harbored second thoughts. Working in the traffic car was like going back in time. It was difficult to remember the details of a radio call unless he wrote everything on a note pad as the call came out. He continually had to ask the radio operator to repeat information he was given. That old self-confident cop was now a scared and worried coward. Howard needed a confidence builder—some positive law enforcement experience to prove that he could still do the job. Weeks went by with no change. Then, the incident that would restore his self-esteem, but in turn damage his relationship with his supervisors, was about to occur. The following is Howard's own account of the event:

No Thanks For Robbery Arrest: "This is an account of a series of incidents that stemmed from my arrest of a bank robbery suspect. It is an illustration of how the repercussions from one incident affected me for over two years. Seventeen years later, it is still difficult for me to discuss these incidents without becoming emotional. The fictitious name of the robbery suspect will be 'Lurch.'

"While working my district on a Friday afternoon, I focused on a bank robbery call that occurred in an adjoining district. I listened carefully to the description of the suspect and positioned myself in an area the robber was likely to pass as he fled. The description was very unique: white male; 20 to 25-years-old; 6 feet 8 inches tall; very thin; hunched shoulders; long curly brown hair; and wearing a black leather jacket, blue jeans, black work boots, and sun glasses. I looked for, and couldn't find, the robber during that work shift. The next day I arrived at my off-duty security job at a bus terminal. Early in the four-hour shift, I observed a tall white male with curly hair and black leather jacket. The man was very thin and stoop-shoul-dered and seemed to fit the description of the robber perfectly. The man picked up a passenger and got into a pickup truck before I had a chance to approach him. Having made note of the license number of the truck, I called the FBI office to give them the information. An agent was able to add to the robber's de-scription, indicating that the black leather jacket had a diago-nal zipper, and the work boots were brand new. This new infor-mation eliminated the man I had just observed leaving the ter-minal.

"Now the unbelievable and unusual happened. About one-half hour before the end of my shift, a very tall, skinny, stoop-shouldered, bushy-haired man, wearing a black leather jacket with diagonal zipper, dark glasses, and new black work boots, purchased a bus ticket. As the man turned from the counter, he saw me and nervously walked to a restaurant portion of the terminal. I followed, and he carefully watched me as he walked back to the general waiting area. At this point, the uncertainty of the situation made me very tense. I had to decide which of the following three options to exercise:

Option #1 Decide that I must be mistaken in my suspi-cions. It would be too much of a coincidence that a bank robber from Friday would walk into me the next day. Take no action at all.

Discussion: Some officers would choose this option be-cause they are either burned out *(lost interest or concern for police work)*, they are lazy, or they are just naive. Choosing this option leaves many criminals free to continue victimizing the innocent.

Option #2 Call for an on-duty backup unit and then arrest the suspect upon their arrival.

Discussion: Although this is the safest option for the officer, this option has some disadvantages. Officers are reluctant to call for a backup unit right away, because of fear of being embarrassed in front of fellow officers if their suspicions are incorrect. This option also opens the way for complaints or false arrest suits if the officer is lacking probable cause to make the arrest.

Option #3 Approach the man and question him concerning his identity and destination. Check his attitude and body language. *(Is he cooperative or nervous?)* After this evaluation of the person, an officer may either: (a) release the man after obtaining enough information to enable detectives to contact him later if necessary; or, (b) arrest the man and transport him to the police precinct for further screening by a supervisor.

Discussion: This option presents the most danger to the officer because of the advantage given to the suspect, but it gives the officer a chance to make additional checks on his/her suspicions before calling for a backup unit, and reduces the chance for embarrassment.

"In making the decision as to which option to choose, I had to quickly imagine all of the possible reactions of the very large and very ugly man. I knew that I would either suffer the consequences of a bad decision or experience the success of a good arrest. I chose Option #3, and approached the ugly man. Our initial conversation was as follows:

"'Sir, would you mind talking to me in the security office?'

"'What for?'

"'I think I recognize you from somewhere, and I want to check your identification.'

"'You can check my ID right here.'

"'I just didn't want to embarrass you.'

"The ugly man got up and towered over my 5 foot 10 inch frame. I took a step backwards, expecting the worst. Now was the time to consider the options that were available to the tall man, if, in fact, he was a criminal.

Criminal's option #1 (RUN) This option is used a great

114

deal by criminals, because they know that the officer is prevented by laws, regulations, and public opinion, from using his firearm.

Criminal's Option #2 (KILL OR DISABLE THE OFFICER) If the criminal is desperate and has nothing to lose, he/she may fight with the officer. If the criminal has a weapon, he/she has the great advantage of surprise. The criminal usually has the opportunity of taking the first shot, and that first shot is sometimes the only shot needed. A man the size of Lurch is capable of overpowering an officer and killing the officer with the officer's own gun.

Criminal's Option #3 (PLAY IT COOL) When criminals choose Option #1 or Option #2, they know they are admitting guilt. Realizing this fact, many criminals continue to cooperate in an attempt to somehow convince the officer of their innocence. Most criminals will cooperate to the point wherein there is no doubt in their mind that they are going to be arrested; and then they will exercise Option #1 or Option #2.

"Taking the ugly man's options into consideration, I began to fear for my safety. Lurch reached into his jeans pocket and pulled out a piece of pictured identification. It was a relief to see that it wasn't a knife or a gun that he pulled from his pocket. It would have been embarrassing to have drawn my police revolver as Lurch reached for his identification. Our next conversation went like this:

"'This is First Avenue identification—It's no good.' *(Lurch started walking toward the front entrance to the terminal, and I thought he was going to run.)*

"'If you don't like my fucking ID, give it back to me.'

"'Do you have any more ID?' *(He handed me a Metro Pass.)*

"'If I'm not under arrest, give my ID back.'

"'I just have to verify that this identification is legitimate.'

"*(As he started to walk out of the terminal, I picked up a pay phone and dialed 911 and whispered)* 'This is off-duty officer Monta, working the bus depot—I would like to see another unit here.'

"'DO YOU NEED A BACKUP?'

"'YES, SOON!'"

"'We will get a car there right away.'

"Fortunately for me, this is the kind of radio call that still prompts a quick response. It was a great relief when, within one or two minutes, two officers entered the terminal. One of the officers said, 'What's his name?' I handed the identification to the officer. That officer said, 'We have a warrant bulletin on this guy out in the car.' I immediately grabbed Lurch and spun him toward the wall, and told him he was under arrest. I attempted to keep Lurch off balance, as he was searched for weapons and handcuffed. The fact that there was now a total of three officers interfered with Lurch's options to fight or run. One of the officers retrieved the bulletin bearing a picture of Lurch from their car. It contained information about a waterfront burglary two months earlier, where Lurch was caught and had fought with officers. Lurch had been booked into jail for the burglary, but he had been released on his personal recognizance pending his trial. *(Why a dirtbag like Lurch was released on his promise to appear for trial is beyond me.)* He had given a flophouse for an address, but that didn't hinder his getting out of jail. As could have been expected, Lurch didn't show for his court hearing; and that is why the $10,000 burglary warrant was issued. My main concern was still more about the bank robbery than about the warrant.

"I talked with an FBI agent by phone. He was anxious to get Lurch into a lineup the following Monday. I called a Robbery Unit detective from my department, and he advised me to book Lurch on the bank robbery charge in addition to the burglary warrant. This would guarantee that Lurch wouldn't be released again before getting him into a lineup and a courtroom. Lurch was advised of his rights, and he was transported by the backup unit to the headquarters write-up room. My shift was now completed at the bus terminal, and I punched out. I was now on my own time—off duty. At the very least, an "Officer's Statement" form was required of me, so I went to the write-up room. The work shift for the backup officers was over. They were anxious to get home. An on-duty police sergeant told me that I could complete the reports and booking for the arrest, so that the other officers could go off duty. This was a reasonable deci-

sion since I had all of the information concerning the bank robbery incident. I would then be on overtime pay. That makes
more sense than having the other two officers working overtime. I worked four and one-half hours on reports, statements,
processing evidence, talking with the FBI, and booking Lurch
into jail. I applied for only four hours of overtime pay, because I
should have been able to complete the paperwork faster. There
were too many interruptions from officers asking about the arrest.

"The booking of Lurch is a story in itself. Lurch had told
me that he was going to do something "weird" if his leather
jacket was taken from him. I mentioned that comment to jail
staff so that they could take measures to protect themselves
when they took Lurch's clothing. A new set of jail rules was in
effect for potential fighters because of the death of a prisoner
who had fought with jailers. A supervisor, a nurse, and three
large jailers were called to assist. Our little group marched
through the jail hallway to the corner of a cellblock. Lurch was
taken behind a temporary partition just out of eyesight of the
nurse. Now think about this weird, silent procession of people
walking through the jail halls. Put yourself in Lurch's place
when they start calling for a nurse and supervisor. Lurch got a
strange look on his face, and he became very cooperative. 'What's
all the fuss?' he said, 'Go ahead and take my jacket.' The entire
clothing change was very tense and silent. Lurch probably
thought they had called for a minister also and were planning
something terrible for him. The rest of the booking was uneventful.

"I went home, very proud—but exhausted. Words cannot
describe the intensity and range of emotions that I experienced
during the five-hour incident. At the conclusion of such an incident, an officer will be on an emotional high but so drained that
it is often difficult to drive home. These symptoms, so I've been
told, are consequences of stress. My stress from this incident
had only begun. The worst was yet to come.

"This successful arrest was especially good for my mental
health, because I had just returned to my police duties after
being off work for three months, recuperating from a serious

head injury. I had crashed on a police motorcycle, crushed my foot, broke my clavicle, and cracked my helmet. I had a concussion that caused a serious loss of memory. My memory returned very slowly. This was my first good arrest after returning to work, and it raised my confidence level out of the gutter.

"I returned to duty on my regular shift on Monday, still feeling pretty proud of myself. I expected a few pats on the back for police work well performed. After all, isn't that what police work is all about? Catching the bad guys? I was stunned when the first comment made by my sergeant was criticism rather than praise. The sergeant told me that I had acted contrary to department procedures for arrests made during off-duty employment. He told me that the arrest should have been turned over to on-duty officers to avoid overtime pay. I tried to explain that I was the only officer present with information and evidence needed to complete the robbery arrest. I told him that I would have been eligible for overtime anyway, because of the time it would have taken to complete the Officer's Statement and brief the other officers.

"The sergeant countered that argument by telling me that the on-duty officers could have booked Lurch on the burglary warrant on Saturday, and the detectives could have investigated Lurch for the robbery on Monday. I told the sergeant that the robbery detective was worried that Lurch might somehow be released on the burglary charge, as had happened once already. The sergeant also told me that I could have waited until Monday to complete the Officer's Statement. *(Department policy indicates that the statement must be completed while the incident is still fresh in the officer's mind.)* I became very upset, because I realized that there was no way to win this argument.

"Out of curiosity, I went to the robbery office to see if any progress had been made with the investigation. Two robbery detectives greeted me and gave me the pat on the back and the compliments I had expected from my sergeant. The detectives said that the FBI had conducted the lineup that same morning. Lurch got into the lineup, glared at the observers and said, 'What the fuck you got me up here for? I did the robbery!!' His public defender attorney came unglued and asked Lurch to say no more.

The detectives also showed me a hidden camera photograph of Lurch at the teller's window. My emotions went from the "lower-than-snake-shit" verge of a nervous breakdown, immediately to another emotional high, brought on by the good news and proper treatment. I blurted out a spontaneous response: 'Thank goodness the arrest was good— That makes up for all the shit I took for the overtime.' The detectives got an astonished look on their faces and I realized I had opened my mouth when I shouldn't have.

"One detective said, 'What do you mean, you got shit over the overtime? That was a hell of an arrest!'

" I said, 'Please just forget what I said. I have to work in my unit for a few more years; I don't need any more trouble.' The detectives pressured me until I told the whole story. I pleaded with them to not let word of my complaining get back to my sergeant, but it was evident that the detectives were not very happy to hear the way I had been rewarded for the arrest. I left the robbery office happy about the successful lineup and the good treatment, but very worried that my complaining might make waves.

"The next day at roll call, the sergeant was still angry, as was I. He told me that while I was working for him, I was to do as I was told, and not get involved in police work while off duty. I asked that he put his order in writing. That statement only created more friction between us. I went out and worked my district with a heavy heart.

"The disappointment with my sergeant weighed heavily on my mind. After a few days we had both cooled off and my depression was starting to lift, but the "shit was about to hit the fan" again. The detectives had talked about the mistreatment that I had suffered. The story had reached their administrators and from there had bounced right back to the captain of my unit. This apparently caused great embarrassment for him and the lieutenant. I was called into the sergeant's office and bitterly admonished for taking this complaint out of the unit. I was invited to transfer to another unit if I didn't like the way he ran his squad, and I was again reminded to keep my nose clean off duty. Once again I was crushed as a result of that one robbery arrest.

"The Lieutenant did everything he could to get around the Captain's promise that I could return to motorcycle duty. He even devised a motorcycle riding test that seemed designed to cause me to fail because of my positional vertigo problem. He and the sergeant watched while I rode the motorcycle into a small circle of traffic cones at slow speed. Then, at a whistle command, I was to tilt my head back and look up at a streetlight while in the tight turn. By some miracle, I managed to remain upright. The Lieutenant reluctantly allowed me back on motorcycle duty. I will admit, now that I am retired, that the Lieutenant was correct in his assessment that I should not have been riding motorcycles with a significant vertigo disability.

"Time passed, and my relationship with the sergeant appeared to normalize, aided by my apology for the embarrassing feedback from the robbery unit. Over the next few months I began to feel that the sergeant and the lieutenant were waiting for me to screw up. During one minor disagreement, the sergeant blew up and screamed that I was crazy. He called me a "stupid shit" and told me to "shut up." I became paranoid, believing that they were determined to get even with me.

"My fears were realized nearly one year after the robbery arrest. I was called to the lieutenant's office. The sergeant was present as the lieutenant asked me to read a "letter of correction" and sign it. The lieutenant told me that he was not criticizing my police work, only choosing not to follow orders given by my supervisor. The letter was, for the most part, a reprimand for not following orders; and it mentioned a quote from my argument with the sergeant about the off-duty bank robbery arrest. One paragraph read, in part, "While you are a police officer twenty-four hours a day, common sense and the police manual both dictate an on-duty and off-duty status for you. Please familiarize yourself with the manual procedures and follow them." The letter went on to accuse me of not following a direct order from my sergeant, but it gave no reference to a specific incident. I respectfully told the lieutenant that the letter was very vague, and I asked if he would identify such an incident. He said that on one occasion, when my unit had a special assignment to escort a dignitary *(vice-presidential candidate Geraldine Ferraro)*, I was told by my sergeant to take care of a Traffic Court case rather than assist my crew with the escort. He accused me of not taking care of the court case.

"I tried to explain that I had appeared at court and was there for about one hour before meeting with the prosecutor and two witnesses to discuss the case. I told the lieutenant that it was determined from that meeting that my testimony was not needed, because I did not witness the accident that was the subject of the trial. The prosecuting attorney told me I was excused and could return to duty. I obtained the location of the motorcycle escort via police radio and caught up with them as soon as I could. The lieutenant said that he had checked the court record and found that I had not testified in the court trial. He told me that I should not have talked my way out of the trial after being ordered to "take care of the court case." I had to admit that if asking the prosecuting attorney whether or not my testimony was needed was considered "talking my way out of a trial," then I was guilty of talking my way out of it. It had taken him a whole year of waiting to get even, and this "trumped-up" accusation was the best he could come up with. He was being pitifully petty, but it must have made him feel better. I was so intimidated by a person with the rank of lieutenant making such serious accusations that I signed the letter without protesting.

"It was only after days of anguish and confusion that I realized what happened in that office was not a normal practice and certainly was not a proper means of disciplining an officer. The letter of correction went on to prohibit me from being a "primary investigating officer" because I was a traffic officer. It read, "Patrol officers have primary investigative responsibility and you will support these officers only. Patrol will do all necessary investigation in incidents in which you become involved." This statement would restrict me from writing police reports. It was most demeaning. If I had followed the lieutenant's order to the letter, I would have developed a reputation within the Patrol Division as the laziest officer in the department. You don't ask other police officers to do your investigative reports for you.

For two years, I wondered what they would think of next. I was continually plagued by a fear that any common mistake that would normally be overlooked if committed by another officer would be used to discipline me.

"During this difficult time, I continued seeing the psychologist. During one day while working on the police bike, my anxiety reached an intolerable level. The doctor had instructed me to come in anytime I felt that way, and he would have an associate screen me for a mood-altering drug. I knew it was time, and while still on duty, I was examined. Once I had a prescription in my pocket, it was like a great pressure was lifted from me. I began taking the drug Ativan. Taking Ativan is the equivalent of dropping out of the world for a period of time. No one should attempt to perform police duties in the relaxed condition that I enjoyed for two weeks. At the beginning of the second day of taking the drug, I stopped for coffee with fellow bike officers Michael T Scott, Jerry Hofstee, and Dick Gagnon. While sipping my coffee, I realized I had not turned my police radio on. I said, 'Oh shit, I forgot to turn my radio on. This darn Ativan has me feeling like I don't know half of what is going on during the day!'

"Dick replied, 'Well, Howard, now you are finally acting normal—You've joined the rest of us.' He was probably correct. I had always been a little overeager and hyperactive.

"It was difficult to continue working while suffering the burden of having been given orders which conflicted with my preconceived image of my profession, and which also conflicted with common sense. I survived the hardship of working for that lieutenant for over two years. I was too hardheaded to ask for a transfer. I would not allow them to force me from my job on motorcycles. The lieutenant left the unit before I did, and I went on to enjoy most of the remainder of my career as a supervisor in the DUI Squad and in Patrol.

"When I left the traffic unit, I showed a copy of my letter of correction to the new captain. *(I was still carrying it in my ticket book.)* I told the captain I wanted him to see what terrible working conditions I had been subjected to. After reading the letter, he placed his hand to his forehead and said, 'I can't believe this—

do you mind if I show it to the major?' The major's reaction was also one of amazement, but they said it was too late then to change anything.

"Fortunately, most administrators are compassionate, and they have concern for the morale of their subordinates. It only takes a few to cause devastating morale problems. The problems follow some abusers to other assignments. Stress created for me by my lieutenant illustrates the consequence of creating a perception of misuse and abuse of power. The tragic fact is that a power-abusing administrator leaves a trail of damaged careers in his/her wake. This problem is as significant today as it was when my law enforcement career began in the 1960s."

Police officers nationwide know all too well that the most painful stress they suffer is a result of disappointment and anger caused by a lack of support from those from whom support is expected. From whom is support expected? It's expected from peers, superiors, other employees in the criminal justice system, and from those who claim to be law-abiding citizens.

The motorcycle accident was the seventh time Howard had narrowly escaped his permanent demise. This time was different than the others. He had gained a realization of the fine line between life and death. He didn't know where he heard the saying about cats having nine lives, but having survived seven near-death events, he began to relate his adventurous life to that of the cat. Howard wondered if he would be granted another two free chances for survival. He was destined to have a number of thrilling close calls after he left motorcycle duty and transferred to a supervisory position in the DUI Squad, and later to supervising a patrol squad.

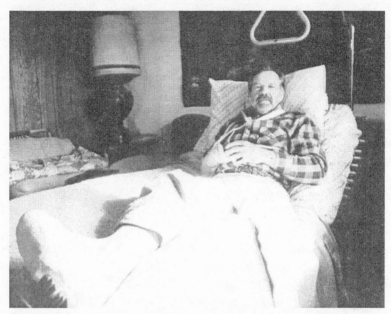

Howard A. Monta recovering from head, shoulder, rib, and foot injuries from police motorcycle accident occuring on October 13, 1983.

CHAPTER 9

Even the Sergeant's Job is Not Safe

Being in uniform and performing police duties on the street was so appealing that Howard was not motivated to seek promotion until he was approaching his twentieth anniversary with SPD. Firefighters and police officers shared the same pension system. His five years of fighting fires combined with his law enforcement career brought Howard close to retirement. It was time to get serious about his financial future and hit the books in preparation for promotional exams. He studied every spare minute, going so far as taking law books to Seattle Mariners baseball games to study between innings. The exceptional effort paid off. Howard was placed second on the promotional list. After giving up his beloved motorcycle assignment, a transfer to a patrol squad in the North Precinct provided valuable experience for a future supervisory assignment. He was promoted to the rank of Sergeant after only nine months in the patrol assignment. During that nine months, and after his promotion, there were many more close calls. Here is Howard's description of one such event:

Woman Attempting "Suicide by Cop"

"It was 1987, five months before my promotion to Police Sergeant. I was a patrol officer assigned to a two-officer car. My partner *(Gary Williams)* and I were dispatched to the home

125

address of a suicidal woman in her late thirties. She reportedly had just picked up a .357-magnum revolver and ammunition, and her intention was to kill her next-door neighbor and herself. We were given a description of the Mazda she was driving. The Mazda was not parked at her residence, but we were able to contact the complainant—her sister. We had just begun to discuss the nature of the problem that had driven the woman to such a mental state, when another officer in our squad *(Phil Rees)* radioed that he was behind the Mazda near our location. Phil radioed that the Mazda was pulling into the alley behind the suspect's residence. I saw the Mazda stop, and I heard the woman yell something unintelligible at her sister. It sounded like profanity. She then sped out of the alley with Phil in hot pursuit. Gary and I ran for our car. The Mazda was at the end of the long block, heading for us at a high rate of speed. Phil was behind with siren and emergency lights operating.

"For some ridiculous reason, my old traffic officer instincts took over. I stepped into the street and signaled for her to stop by holding the palm of my hand toward her. I have often looked back and criticized myself for such a stupid act. As could have been predicted from a suicidal person, she swerved the car right at me, and I had to jump behind the parked police car to avoid being hit. What I would not have predicted is that she slammed on her brakes and slid to a stop just a few feet from us.

"Gary was two steps ahead of me as we approached the driver's door. We were about six feet from the door when I saw the woman reach for a large gun that was in plain view on the passenger seat. My first instinct was to dive behind the police car for cover, but Gary had a different idea. He dove right into the driver's side window of that little Mazda and sprawled across the woman's lap. I was astonished, partly because I couldn't figure out how Gary fit himself into the window. To put it politely, he is a big guy. Then I became very worried for Gary. I ran to the passenger side, and while focusing my gun on the woman, I tried to open the door. It was locked. I could see that the woman had the revolver in her hand, and Gary was struggling to hold her hand down on the seat. My decision to use deadly force had been made, but Gary's body was across her body, and I did not have a good shot. I waited for what seemed like forever for Gary to either wrestle the gun away from her or for him to move enough for me to get a shot at her. There was no way to accurately describe my state of mind in that situation, knowing that my partner and I could be shot, or that I might have to kill the woman.

"It seemed like a miracle had occurred when Gary took possession of the revolver and struggled to extract himself from the window. There was some difficulty prying the woman from her car, but it was nothing compared to the ordeal we had just experienced. Gary saved me from having to be an executioner. A letter of commendation was submitted for his brave act. I would have kissed him if I thought he wouldn't have punched me out for doing so. As is common in similar situations, a good night's sleep was not to be had for over a week. The nightmares persisted, and I would continue to dream about being involved in a shootout with desperate criminals."

This was not what Howard would consider a near-death experience, but the lives of both officers were certainly placed in jeopardy by the disturbed woman.

Another hair-raising adventure occurred just prior to Howard's promotion to Sergeant. He was working a two-man car with an old friend and partner *(Tom Sutton)* whom he had worked with while assigned to motorcycles—and who also had suffered a near-fatal motorcycle accident. This is one call that neither of them will forget. They were in the Ballard area of Seattle, looking for a suspect who had just pushed a Harley Davidson motorcycle out of the owner's yard. Apparently, the thief had coasted it about six blocks, to where he had parked a pickup truck. When the officers found him, he was attempting to push the large motorcycle up a ramp to the truck bed. As Howard left the patrol car, the thief took off running. Howard had been jogging since his fire-fighting days, and there was no way that Tom was going to be able to join that foot pursuit. Howard yelled at Tom to broadcast their location and to keep an eye on the motorcycle. The predator and his prey ran through yards and over fences for five blocks. Howard lost sight of the thief momentarily and stood quietly while peering over a fence, trying to determine his direction of travel. Then he noticed the suspect peeking around the corner of a garage trying to see where the crazy cop was. The chase was on again. Howard was trying to scream his location on his portable radio, but he was only guessing where he was.

After about three more blocks, they ran into a schoolyard. The thief was tired, and he dropped to his hands and knees in the middle of the schoolyard. Howard jumped on his back, shouting at him to get flat on his stomach and put his hands behind him. With a radio in his right hand and a gun in his left hand, Howard had difficulty controlling the flailing suspect. During an attempt to put the radio in his belt holder, the radio fell to the ground. The crook began to rise to his feet, attempting to throw the worried cop from his back. It was later discovered that the thief had been a weightlifter in prison and had just recently been released on parole (for an Auto Theft conviction). Howard forced him back to the ground on his hands and knees once again, but the incredibly strong man again rose up with the cop on his back. As strong as Howard was, he was thinking the worst, and worry was quickly turning to terror. He didn't want to shoot the guy, but he feared the desperate man would take his gun away from him.

In panic, Howard started striking the suspect behind his left ear with the 38-caliber Smith & Wesson revolver. They dropped to the ground again. This time the thief picked up the portable radio and broadcast for all officers on the north frequency to hear, "Someone help me, this cop is beating me with his gun!"

Howard screamed at him, "I'm going to shoot you with my gun if you don't stay down." The bewildered crook must have thought that Howard was "nuts"—he stopped resisting and submitted to handcuffs. Howard had some difficulty living down the comments that were made on his radio by that motorcycle thief. That had to be one of the most unusual police-radio broadcasts in history. The rules and regulations prohibited officers from striking a person on the head unless there were circumstances that would justify the use of deadly force. If the administration of the police department would have chosen to discipline Howard for using excessive force, he was prepared to accept whatever criticism or penalties were deemed appropriate. During the confrontation on the school grounds, help was not in sight. Howard had always maintained that if a cop is involved in a one-on-one physical confrontation, the adversary has as much access to the cop's gun as the cop does. He firmly believed that if others could have put themselves in his shoes in such a violent struggle, they would have used whatever force necessary to survive. Howard didn't get in trouble for his actions on that day, but he did not escape entirely unscathed. His partner *(Tom)* and many other cops were able to have a good laugh at his expense.

Howard's first supervisory assignment as a new sergeant was Seattle's DUI Squad. He was a little disappointed, because he had been assigned to the Traffic Section for almost his entire career. He tolerated the move because he knew it would not restrict his aggressive law enforcement style. Just as he found he was able to catch criminals while he was assigned to motorcycles *(rather than just write speeding tickets)*, he knew he could continue the hunt for criminals. He did worry a little about his old drinking buddy from the sixties turning over in his grave if he were aware that Howard was supervising a DUI Squad. He knew exactly what Dick Rae would say to him: "It takes one to catch one." Howard had already quit drinking alcoholic beverages; however, his sudden sobriety was not by choice. After his severe head injury from the motorcycle accident, his tolerance level for alcohol had dropped to zero. He couldn't even enjoy a glass of wine with a meal without suffering debilitating depression for days after. If he had not already given up drinking before his new assignment, Howard always said that after two years of witnessing the misery that alcohol creates for people and their families, he would have stopped drinking anyway.

To make the new job even more interesting, the former sergeant of the squad had enticed the department administration to equip the officers and sergeant with 1985, 5-liter Ford Mustangs. The logic of the ex-supervisor was that drunks would be less likely to attempt to engage in evasive action if officers were able to close the distance between them rapidly. Whatever prompted the department administration to buy the Mustangs for his squad, Howard was thankful.

The following high-speed chase accurately depicts Howard's enthusiasm for his new assignment, and for his Mustang:

"A Shot In The Groin Justifies All-Out Chase" is what I call this story. The car pursuit involved in the incident would have terminated if there had not been a shooting involved. During my 1988-89 tour of duty supervising Seattle's DUI Squad, I had the pleasure of driving a 5-liter Ford Mustang. That was the first hot car that Seattle PD had used since the 1970 Plymouth Satellite, with the "440" engine.

"At 2:30 a.m., I was doing paperwork in my office at Headquarters in the downtown area. I overheard a call of a shooting on the North End radio frequency. The suspects in the shooting matched the description of suspects in an attempted robbery in North Seattle which occurred at about 1:00 a.m. Earlier in the evening, the same group had been involved in a robbery in Kent, Washington, where they had outrun a police pursuit in a big-block, Green 1979 Chevrolet Camaro. Although the shooting was 10 to 12 miles from my location, a little lighted sign flashed in my brain that said, *I could catch these guys.*

"I speculated that they might be South-End residents, since they had been in Kent earlier. One could either sit southbound on Interstate 5 and watch for them to go by, or another option would be to cruise out Aurora Avenue North *(Highway 99)* and meet them halfway. My choice of Aurora Avenue proved to be correct. While northbound on Aurora at N 87th Street, about fifteen minutes after the shooting, a green Camaro passed by me going southbound. The driver was a white male in his twenties, the passenger a black male in his thirties, and there were two young females in the back seat—just like the description of the suspects that was broadcast.

"I made a U-turn and told police radio to get backup units for me. The Camaro driver continued at normal speed for about ten blocks. My emergency equipment had not been actuated yet, because I was waiting for some help. When the driver ran red lights at N 75th Street, and at Winona Avenue, the chase was on. We accelerated to over 100 mph as we entered the divided portion of Highway 99. I was screaming my location, hoping for help that I knew would not be able to match our speed anyway. There was that ominous feeling that at the end of this chase there would probably be a shootout with these two crazies in the Camaro, and then I would face them all alone. We were approaching the Battery Street Tunnel entrance in the downtown area, and traveling over 100 mph. Six blocks from the tunnel, an ambitious patrol officer attempted to pull out from a side street as the Camaro was about to pass by him. For some reason, the patrol car lost a rear wheel and started swerving as it was entering the tunnel. I was closing on him rapidly and had to slow to avoid the patrol car and the wheel that was rolling in the traffic lane.

"The Camaro was out of view when I exited the tunnel and traveled onto the Alaskan Way Viaduct. Headlights of only a few slow-moving cars were ahead of me. I continued at 100 mph and peered ahead. Finally, the Camaro came into view about a mile in front of me, with headlights off. He was passing 60-mph traffic as if other cars were standing still. I could only hope he had not taken the Kingdome off ramp, as I blew by it. Rounding a curve leaving the elevated portion of the viaduct, I could not see the Camaro ahead of me. I caught a glimpse of the Camaro on the railroad tracks to my right out of the corner of my eye. He had turned off the roadway and high centered on the tracks. It took me about three blocks to get my car stopped. Four figures were leaving the Camaro, headed westbound toward the piers on Puget Sound. Patrol Units from Seattle's South Precinct had been rolling my way, and they picked up the two females on the surface street within two minutes.

"A K-9 Unit was called to search for the males. Inside the Camaro was a loaded, sawed-off shotgun between the front bucket seats. Facing that weapon, and the other weapon(s) possessed by the robbers, by myself would have been pure hell. A search dog was checking a fenced storage area on one of the piers and located the black male suspect in a tool shed. The dog jumped on the suspect as he reached into a leather bag containing two handguns. That was a lucky K-9 officer. We finally had to give up on the search for the white male driver. We were hoping that the detectives would be able to identify him by questioning the other suspects, or by the contents of the Camaro.

"The driver was eventually identified. I was subpoenaed to testify at the trial held for both suspects. While waiting in the courthouse lobby to be called to testify, the victim, who had been shot in the groin, came out of the courtroom. He was amused. He seemed to have recovered with no complaints of permanent injury. For some reason he wanted to share with the officers what had amused him in the courtroom. He said, 'They asked me where I was hit by the bullet, and I told them, 'Right in the dick.'"

"*Kind of rude and crude,* I thought. I wonder what the jury thought of that answer. Apparently, the victim was robbed outside a tavern where he had met with the suspects for "some matter." *(Could it have been drugs?)* He was shot because he resisted giving up his money. We found out at trial how the white male suspect had escaped the manhunt. He jumped into Puget Sound from a pier. He grabbed a passing tugboat and was towed to the Harbor Island industrial area *(about one mile south)*. He ended up—wet, shaking and cold—at the door of a friend in West Seattle. That friend testified at the trial. The two suspects were found guilty of First-Degree Assault, and both were sentenced to about five years in prison. By now, they are probably out victimizing the public again. Chalk one up for the 5-liter Mustang."

Even on the quiet nights, there was always the chance of something terrible happening. Howard was supervising his crew in the vicinity of 15th Avenue West, a major six-lane thoroughfare that leads from downtown to the Ballard area of Seattle. It was 11 p.m. on the Saturday before Halloween, and the DUI Squad expected alcoholic beverages would be abused all over the city. Howard was parked on a side street that angles onto the thoroughfare, watching for errant drivers, making himself available to his squad if needed. The Mustang was parallel parked at the curb, between other cars. An older four-door sedan appeared in his left rear-view mirror. It was accelerating unusually rapidly to merge with the traffic on 15th West. The car was also swerving erratically back and forth as it approached the parked police car. That familiar, onerous feeling that the worst was about to happen overcame Howard. As the sedan neared, it swerved violently toward the parked cars. Howard tucked his chin down to his chest and braced himself for a violent collision. He couldn't take his eyes off of the mirror. The sedan struck the rear fender of a beautiful black Buick behind him. It bounced off the Buick, then veered sharply back to the right and struck the driver's-side door of the police Mustang with great force.

Even though the police vehicle was in parking gear, it was knocked across the sidewalk, and a full car length ahead. Howard was trying to regain his composure so that he could attempt to chase his attacker if the sedan didn't stop. It did pull over into the next driveway that led to an apartment building parking lot. Shook up, but with no apparent broken bones, Howard struggled out of the Mustang. He cautiously approached the mangled sedan, and was greeted by a slurred, but sweet voice. "Hi, officer. I was just on my way to a Halloween party. I guess I'm not going to make it." Not only did she have that blank, *What? Me worry?* look on her face, her voice sounded like her tongue was swollen to twice its normal size—all the signs of an intoxicated driver. Howard had called for a member of the DUI Squad to come to his assistance. It was a sight to behold for passing motorists when the DUI officer was testing the twenty-year-old woman in a beautiful little witch's costume. The forlorn sergeant was taken to the hospital for x-rays. He was sore for a couple of weeks.

Howard should have known that area was trouble for him. A few months before being struck by the witch, he was in the same area, at the same time, when a robber found him. Here is what Howard said about the arrest in his written statement for the Robbery Unit detectives:

"On 06-28-88, at approximately 2329 hours, I was in the vicinity of 15th Avenue West and West Garfield Street assisting

Unit Tom-75 with a DUI arrest. I received a police radio call concerning a robbery and abduction in the Queen Anne area. A vehicle involved was described as being a gold van with a sleeper compartment on top. Within minutes of the radio broadcast, I observed a van northbound on 15th Avenue from Elliott Avenue West. The van was a Dodge with an additional add-on unit on top. The top was white, the body was a metallic brown, with a white stripe. I made a U-turn and followed northbound to Armour Street. The van was being driven very hesitantly, as though the driver wasn't sure of where he was going.

"The van then turned northbound into an alley, which is the access to addresses in the 2800 block of 15th Avenue West. When the van reached a dead end, I put my spotlight into the van windows, and a large white male, about thirty years old, six feet plus, and approximately three-hundred pounds, exited the van from the passenger side. He walked eastbound, up a stairway on the south side of an apartment building. I yelled at him to wait, but he continued. A white male, about twenty-five, five foot eleven, and slim, exited the driver's side with his hands over his head. I saw officers coming up in back of me. I told them to control the driver, and I ran up the stairway after the large man. I momentarily lost sight of him at the top of the stairway and then caught sight of him running northbound on the east sidewalk of 14th Ave., W.

"I continued my pursuit, and cornered him at a rock bulkhead about two hundred feet north of the stairway. He was slow in responding to my command to put his hands up on the rockery. The large male had a cast on his left arm, nearly up to his elbow; and he was difficult to handcuff. I read Miranda warnings from my MIR Card, and he answered 'Yes' to understanding. When asked if he wanted to continue to answer any questions concerning the arrest after considering his rights, he asked, 'What kind of questions?'

"I told the man that I would ask questions like, 'Where did you throw the gun?'

"He replied, 'I did not have a gun to throw.'

"I asked, 'Did you possess something that someone might mistake to be a gun?'

"'I had a sawed off baseball bat,' he answered. When I asked where the bat was, and if it was still in the van, he did not reply." *(End of statement)*

Howard went back later and found a sawed-off 22-caliber rifle in a berry patch. The driver turned out to be the victim of the robbery. He had dropped his live-in girlfriend at their doorstep and was parking his van as she watched. The heavyset robber walked up and pointed the gun at him, saying, "Get in and drive." While the victim was driving, the suspect pointed the rifle at him, and said, "Don't look at me. Just drive me to the Ballard Locks." The robber put the rifle to the victim's head, and then to his knee, threatening, "I'll blow your kneecap off if you don't give me your money." He gave the robber his card case, containing a bankcard, a library card, and his driver's license. The card case was still in the robber's possession when he was arrested. The victim gave his cash machine identification number. Even though he cooperated, he was struck on the right side of his head by the barrel of the gun. The robber also fired three shots inside the van to impress the terrified driver. It is a wonder that the poor excuse for a human being didn't attempt to ambush Howard on the stairway. That was just one more confirmation of Howard's theory that the meanest and nastiest of bullies melt like butter when the odds are even— just like in his old high school days.

After two years with the DUI Squad, the good sergeant was happy for the opportunity to transfer to a Patrol Sector at the North Precinct. Nothing changed for him—a fact that the next adventure will substantiate.

Actual Kidnap or Extortion Attempt? What Howard thought was going to be one of the greatest investigations of his career, his most significant triumph over the criminal element, turned out to be a devastating letdown. This event resembled the comedic script of a bad play.

In May 1992, a very successful businesswoman received a call from her 28-year-old brother *(fictitious name "John")*. John had a history of drug abuse. He told his sister that he had stolen some money from a "bad dude," and that he was being held for $2,000 ransom in a downtown hotel room. John told her that he would be killed if the persons holding him at gunpoint did not receive the money by 6 p.m. The woman received seven calls between 8:30 a.m. and 5:15 p.m. The ransom demand rose to a high of $3,100. The woman was hesitant to involve the police, because there was some doubt in her mind that her brother was actually abducted, and she feared involving police might jeopardize her brother's safety if he was not faking.

It was after 4:00 p.m. when the first officer arrived to investigate the complaint. That officer called Howard to supervise the investigation as soon as he learned the serious nature of the call. Howard was informed that the officer had already notified the detective unit that would normally follow-up on this type of investigation. *(Homicide and Robbery)* It was surprising to hear they were not going to respond, and that they had instructed the officer to just forward a report to their office. Police radio silence was requested in case the persons involved might have access to a scanner. One of the suspects called the woman just after Howard's arrival. The caller was screaming about killing her brother if she would not come up with the money. Howard instructed the woman to bargain the demand down. She told the suspect she could not come up with the amount they were asking by 6:00 p.m. He told her he needed $2,000 by 9:00 p.m. at the latest. She negotiated with two different suspects during several phone conversations while the Police Communications Unit officers were working with the telephone company to trace the calls.

At one point, both suspects changed the story to include that her brother had been involved in "a drug deal gone bad," and that "Our Mexican friends will kill your brother for sure if they are not paid." Howard told the woman that she could set up a money drop for $500 at a public place in the Ballard area that police could stake out, but it would have to be her decision. She wanted to do it, so when the suspect called back at 8:30 p.m., she made arrangements to meet the suspect with $500 in the meat department of a local grocery store. She told him she would not give him the partial payment unless she could see that her brother was all right. They went for the deal.

Howard borrowed jackets for two officers to put over their uniforms, and the officers sat in a plain car in the grocery store lot. Marked patrol units were scattered and hidden all around the area. It was not long after the trap was set that the officers in the store lot broadcast information that a taxicab carrying five persons had arrived. They said three persons walked into the store. The woman later told Howard that her brother and two suspects met her in the meat department. She said that one suspect opened his coat and showed her a sawed-off rifle in a holster while demanding the $500 ransom. The three got nervous when the woman insisted that her brother be released to her, and they fled the store. By this time all police units were converging on the store. As Howard approached, he saw two men running. He managed to contain one, while the other disappeared down a dark walkway.

To his surprise, the guy Howard had detained was the woman's brother. He was trying to act as though his life had just been saved. He was a poor actor. Howard asked him, "If you didn't want to be around those guys, why were you running away from the store with them?" His only explanation was that he was afraid. The dark walkway where the suspect had disappeared was checked, and a sawed-off 22-caliber rifle and holster were found. The brother and two others were arrested for Attempted Extortion. Howard made it his personal quest to find the suspect who got away. He talked with a number of local "bad actors" and found out which downtown hotel this group had been operating from. One hotel clerk gave Howard information that enabled him to find the name and date of birth of the missing suspect.

As it turned out, that suspect headed for California the next day. Detectives were able to determine, as officers had expected, that the victim's brother had been a party to the extortion attempt. The whole thing had been staged. The "no justice" aspect of this case is that detectives inactivated the case, and charges were never filed against anyone. For the citizens of Seattle, the only good thing to come out of all of the work and overtime involved was that the guy who fled to California stayed away. He ended up victimizing the good citizens of South Carolina, where in 1995 he was arrested for Check Fraud, and in 1996 for Grand Larceny. He probably thinks he is still wanted for investigation of Kidnap and Extortion in Washington State. Howard was disappointed that the woman's brother was never charged with a crime for endangering so many people. That fool with the rifle could have panicked and fired at Howard while running in the dark walkway.

Never Let Your Guard Down / There's A Crook Around Every Corner. Another spectacular supervisory contribution occurred when Howard was called to the scene of a brutal stabbing in a trailer court near the city limits on Highway 99. When officers arrived, they found a male, twenty-five, on the stairway to the trailer, bleeding profusely from three stab wounds to his chest. He told officers that the man who stabbed him, an acquaintance he knew only by a nickname, had fled the area. Information received from police radio was that witnesses had seen the suspect run southbound on Aurora, and that he lived in a motel in that direction. The Medic Unit had already taken the seriously injured man to the hospital. There was blood all over the trailer. Using the police radio to call for the Homicide Unit to respond would have drawn television and newspaper reporters, thus adding to the difficulty of the investigation.

The phone in the trailer was bloody; and not wanting to disturb the crime scene, Howard started checking neighboring trailers to see if someone would let him use their telephone. No one was at home in the first two trailers. A 36-year-old male came out and greeted him at the third trailer from the stabbing scene. The sergeant told the occupant there had been a stabbing at a neighboring trailer, and that he needed to use a phone. He said, "Just a minute," and after going inside for a few seconds, he returned and held out a cordless phone. As Howard reached for the phone, the trailer occupant said, "I stabbed the guy." Talk about the unexpected! Howard was nearly shocked out of his shoes but quickly stopped the admitted assailant so that Miranda rights could be read.

Instead of handing over the telephone, this man could have

easily poked a knife under Howard's bulletproof vest. It was a great experience for a woman who was riding along as a civilian observer with the sergeant *(a police candidate)*. She is now a valued employee of a Central Washington police department. The lesson learned is that a cop can never let his/her guard down. Howard was one lucky cop *(again)*.

Our hero was far overdue for an encounter that exceeded the close calls. Another such perilous adventure occurred near the end of his shift, in the Lake City area of Seattle. This violent episode was not only Howard's near-death experience number eight, it will illustrate the tension and strain that cops endure when the use of deadly force is imminent. The process of making the decision to take a life is nearly as emotionally damaging as actually having to commit the act.

Jealous Man Holding Two Kids at Knifepoint. Howard was called to an apartment building in the Lake City area of Seattle to supervise officers who were unable to gain the cooperation of a distraught father. He was threatening to kill his children and himself because the mother of his children *(not his wife)* was "fooling around with another guy."

When Howard arrived, he found the second-floor apartment door open. At the far side of the living room, the thirty-year-old male was kneeling on the floor with his arms around two small kids and a butcher knife in each hand. Two officers were pleading with him to let the children go. Howard called for additional units and a hostage negotiator. They continued an attempt to establish a rapport with the crazed man. He didn't want to live anymore because his girlfriend was trying to break off her relationship with him. After meeting him, it did not take much imagination to see why she wanted to get away from him—he was nuts! He kept insisting that he would let the kids go if officers would bring his girlfriend to him. Howard begged him to let the children go so that he could take them to safety, telling him, "I know you love your boys, and you don't want them harmed." He promised that officers would not rush at him if he let the boys go. After considerable coaxing, he released the kids, and they ran to officers waiting in the hallway. He told officers that he was going to kill his girlfriend if he ever could get his hands on her.

As the negotiating continued with the man, an officer thought she was doing a good thing by bringing the man's mother into the room behind the officers. He went berserk, screaming at her, "You knew all this was going on! You knew Sheila was seeing that other guy and you encouraged it!" He got to his feet and raised both butcher knives above his head. Howard yelled at officers to retreat to the hallway with the mother. He had his gun trained on the madman as he backed toward the door. The knife-wielding man continued his advance. Howard told him to stop or he would have to shoot him. The disturbed man said, "That's what I want you to do."

When Howard reached the door, he had to push others into the hall. He slammed the door just as the would-be killer nearly reached him. Howard trained his gun on the door in anticipation of the suspect charging out of the apartment. Howard knew then that he would have to kill the man in order to protect others and himself. He ordered officers to retreat to doorways at both ends of the hallway and told officers at the north end to occupy the stairway above and below the second floor level. This was done to avoid a crossfire situation in the hall, so that no officer would be in another's line of fire. Howard positioned himself at the south end of the hallway, to maintain a watch on the man's apartment door.

By this time, Howard had called for a Lieutenant and the Emergency Response Team *(SWAT)*. As more officers arrived, a two-officer unit was assigned outside the apartment, in case he jumped from his balcony. A negotiator told the radio operator to call inside and ask the man to enter the hallway without the knives. He came out, with butcher knives in his hands. From his position at the end of the hallway, Howard told him to drop the knives and lay down on the floor. His eyes grew big and bulgy, and he charged down the hallway toward the well-meaning sergeant. The now suicidal man raised his right arm and threw a knife at Howard, who stepped back into the stairwell and slammed the fire door. They heard the knife hit the door hard. It could just as well have been sticking out of Howard's neck, or between his eyes. The man's apartment door then slammed shut.

A total of four hours passed. Some pleading was accomplished by phone, and some by shouting back and forth through the apartment door. The negotiators were not making any headway. The crazed man seemed to enjoy the power that he was holding over the cops. The Emergency Response Team had assembled, and they were setting up their command post. Howard's crew was very close to being relieved from their stressful duties, but relief for them was not to be!

A radio transmission was heard from one of the containment officers outside, "He's jumping off the balcony." Howard ran down the stairs and to the front of the apartment building. The wide-eyed man, still clutching two butcher knives, was nearly surrounded on the sidewalk by four officers. The sergeant joined his crew, ensuring that no one was in the line of fire of any officer. Each of them was in extreme jeopardy of being charged by the knife-wielding man, but they could not allow him to run off into the night. There was no doubt in Howard's mind that the man would injure or kill someone if he escaped. Howard told him, "The talking is over—You've played all your cards—One step in any direction and we will have to kill you." What he was telling him was not a bluff; and from the astonished look on his face, Howard thought the distraught man knew he was not bluffing. After a slight hesitation, he carefully placed both knives on the sidewalk. He cooperated from that point on.

During those moments when the use of deadly force was imminent, Howard had experienced another one of those "out of body" occurrences. Once again, it was as if everything were happening in slow motion, and he was functioning on "automatic pilot." He would have killed that man before allowing him to have taken one-half step in any direction. Then Howard would have had trouble living with himself, because he didn't even fish or hunt. He couldn't even kill a spider. At roll call the next day, he asked if anybody had trouble sleeping. Several officers raised their hand. They talked about it for a while. That helped a little. Howard suffered the effects of that event for many weeks. Those horrible dreams of shootouts continued.

Not all of his exciting adventures and close calls occurred as a result of his duty-related patrolling. Howard could not avoid adversity, even while off duty.

CHAPTER 10

Never Really Off Duty

Howard was meticulous about carrying his old Colt 9-mm semi-automatic pistol when he was in public, not because he was afraid for himself, but because of his concern for others. There was one other motivation for his obsessive behavior. Long ago, Howard had developed the frame of mind that he would not allow himself to be victimized without a fight. Ever since Jerry Wyant was killed in the police motorcycle accident, the event that would end Howard's life became a significant issue for him. Wyant died while doing what he loved. As a young man, Howard told his wife that he would never cheat on her for two reasons. The first was that he loved and respected her, and the second was that the most unacceptable manner for him to reach his demise would be to be shot in the back by a jealous husband or boyfriend. He never had a fear of death, but if he had to go, he always said that he would not mind dying in a shootout with criminals—the old "going out in a blaze of glory" routine.

Not only is it the expectation of the employing jurisdiction that police officers exercise their authority twenty-four hours a day, on or off duty, the officers burden themselves by internalizing that responsibility. Taking care of everyone's problems becomes a way of life for cops. Consequently, it is difficult to relax during common, everyday activities such as eating in restaurants, grocery shopping, going to the movies, walking or jogging for health, and visiting neighbors and friends.

Howard could never turn off his uncanny ability to recognize people and things that were suspicious. This trait caused him to be involved in many exciting and dangerous adventures. One night in the late 1980s, Howard and his wife Liz had enjoyed an evening at a dance club. Afterward, they stopped at a 24-hour restaurant on Aurora Avenue. The restaurant was busy, considering the late hour and that it was a weekday. They had a window booth and, as is typical for cops, Howard was seated so that he could view the entryway. They were engaged in heavy conversation about their dance lessons while waiting for breakfast to be served, when Howard noticed an African-American male in his late twenties walking through the parking lot from Aurora.

Any movement in a parking lot caused Howard to become alert for car prowlers. This guy did not approach any cars, and he entered the restaurant. Howard's attention returned to their conversation. When the man remained at the cash register, ignoring the **Please Seat Yourself** sign, Howard refocused his attention. He noticed that the man kept his right hand in his overcoat pocket, and that he continually kept looking at the parking lot and around the restaurant. He could innocently be waiting to ask a cashier for change or directions, or he could be waiting to rob the restaurant. The man's nervous demeanor caused Howard to suspect the latter. Just to critique his own judgement, and to ensure that he had not slipped into the unacceptable practice of "racial profiling," he told Liz, "Turn around and tell me what you think that guy is doing by the cash register."

Surprised by the request, she swung her legs into the aisle and turned to look. She responded, "I think he is going to rob this place." That was all the confirmation he needed.

As he walked away from their booth, Howard told his wife, "Get under the table if guns come out." There was one problem. Having great respect for guns, Howard did not carry a round in the chamber of his Colt. That meant that if he had to fire the pistol, he would first have to pull the barrel back on the slide to eject a round from the clip into the chamber. That would put him at a distinct disadvantage when facing someone who is prepared to shoot him. The would-be robber watched him closely as Howard entered a restroom just behind the cash register. He walked to a far stall, closed the door, and took the semi-auto from its holster. He very gingerly cranked a round into the chamber. *How would I ever explain an accidental discharge in the restroom,* he thought. The gun was ready, and so was Howard. He exited the restroom and stood near the payphone. He was about ten feet behind the man who had been acting so suspiciously. Howard had his hand on the Colt inside his jacket, as he positioned himself between the would-be robber and the exit door. The man looked back nervously several times.

A female employee approached the cash register, asking, "Can I help you?"

The man hesitated and stuttered, "N-N-No— I changed my mind." He turned around and walked out. Howard's first inclination was to jump on him, but he thought, *With my luck he would have been faking a gun in his coat pocket. Then who in the hell would believe my suspicion that he intended to rob the place?* At least he prevented a robbery. That would have to be good enough.

The next two off-duty events are told in Howard's own words:

"Cops in Seattle who were unfortunate enough to be assigned to the old downtown precinct were given no special consideration for personal parking. For the period of time that I was assigned there, I was forced to park about six blocks from the precinct. Because I did not have an AM/FM radio in my old Camaro, I carried my portable police radio for something to listen to while commuting. I left work about 7:00 p.m. one evening in late fall. It was getting dark when I walked to my car through an area that could be described as "not one of the safest areas" of downtown.

"I was always alert to my surroundings, because no one would ever suspect that I was a cop. Dressed in my old coat and jeans, I looked like an easy mark for criminals. Walking past the Courthouse Park, two ugly guys in their twenties vacated a park bench and started following closely behind me. I refer to them as ugly because they were filthy and unshaven. There were not many people around. I was uneasy. A couple of blocks later, they were still on my heels. Picking up my pace to a jog, I hurried toward a traffic signal that was about to change. I made it across the avenue, noticing that my followers continued behind me. We were approaching an even more uninhabited area that consisted mostly of parking lots and old deserted buildings. I pulled my off-duty 9-mm automatic out of the belt holster and discreetly put the gun in my coat pocket. I did so to enable me to keep my hand on the gun. My anxiety level had reached a new record high. I knew that if I were ever to become the victim of a robbery, and was lucky enough to live through it, my fellow cops would never let me live it down.

"I decided to leave the sidewalk and force the two nasty-looking men to commit themselves. *(In other words, "defecate or get off the pot.")* The motions I made to remove the gun from its holster must have made them uneasy. Crooks tend to avoid self-confident prey. They hesitated, and then continued to the next corner. I kept my eye on them as I climbed up hill another block to reach my car.

"As I drove back down the hill, I observed one of the guys standing on the corner. I thought the other guy must have broken into an adjacent old building. The guy on the corner was going through the old "looking-up-and-down-the-block" routine. I slowed to a near stop, looking for the second man. Noticing movement in the back of a parked car to my left, I stopped behind it. The car door opened, and the second man crawled out onto the sidewalk. He got up and both men ran. I used my portable police radio to tell our dispatcher that I was off duty and following two car prowlers into the International District. Police units were dispatched.

The thieves noticed me following them. *(Now the tables were turned.)* They crossed a side street and headed toward a doorway to what looked like a small office building. I aimed my car at the sidewalk and squealed to a stop near the building stairway. The door to the building was locked. They were trapped like rats. *(Remember what they say about "cornered rats.")* I jumped out of my car with my gun in my left hand and my police radio in my right, shouting my location to the radio dispatcher. I yelled to the pair of trapped rats, "I'm a police officer. Get your hands against the wall."

"To my bewilderment, neither of them obeyed my command. The larger and meaner looking of the two turned toward me. His jacket opened, exposing the top of a sizable hunting knife. This was not the first, and was not to be the last, time I would say to myself, *Why me? Why do I get myself into these dilemmas?*

"The guy with the knife said, 'Show us your badge— How do we know you are a cop?' He started toward me.

"My eyes got big and my voice strained as I said, 'Look, asshole, I've got a gun in this hand and a police radio in the other, and I don't have any more hands to show you my fucking badge— Get your hands on that wall or I'll blow your brains all over the stairway!' The idiot hesitated, and he was still trying to make up his feeble mind when two police cars screamed around the corner to save me.

"No dinner for me that night. I called home and told Liz, 'Put the food away— I'm working overtime again!' The paperwork only took me about an hour and a half. The men were charged with Attempt Theft / Vehicle Prowl. The big guy was also charged with Carrying a Concealed Weapon.

"The City won the weapons charge in court, but the car prowl charges were dropped because we never were able to get in touch with the owner of the car. Testimony was necessary to indicate that the big guy didn't have permission to enter the car. This dangerous man got off too easy. There had been a rash of "knife-point street robberies" in the downtown area perpetrated by a criminal who fit the description of the big guy I had arrested. The detectives suspected him, but they were never able to connect him to the robberies. I guess I should have acted more defenseless when he was stalking me. Then I could have finally realized one of my recurring dreams—to see the surprised expression on the face of a criminal who is attempting to victimize me. Of course, I could have ended up with my throat cut."

"Then there was the time that I was driving back from an enjoyable dinner with my wife. Throughout that day, there had been a series of thefts from service stations and stores by a man about my age who was driving a stolen pickup truck. We were nearly home when I made a sudden turn that caused Liz to say, 'What are you doing?'

"I answered, 'That is a stolen truck in front of us. We have been looking for this guy all day.'

"She replied, 'Oh, no! not again!' I told her that I was going to follow the guy until he stopped somewhere and then grab him. Liz was upset with me, but I couldn't resist. We didn't have to go too far out of our way. He stopped at our neighborhood grocery store to steal some beer. I was able to use the phone while he lurked around the store, and I only had to confront him for a short while by myself until a big on-duty cop arrived."

Howard moved to the Ballard neighborhood of Seattle in 1980. It seemed to be such a clean and quiet neighborhood, and he and Liz were eager to move in. They were settled only a few days when neighbors who noticed Howard was a cop *(because of the police motorcycle he drove home daily)* started telling him of the sixteen-year-old on the corner who was a "bad seed." The kid, named Brad *(fictitious name)*, walked up the sidewalk throwing objects at neighboring houses to intimidate the residents. He dared them to challenge him. It was not necessary for Howard to have a heart-to-heart talk with the kid, as he had planned to do. The incorrigible brat caught on right away that a cop was in the neighborhood, and he became a model citizen around home. However, he did not change his errant ways when away from the neighborhood. Within a couple of months, Brad was arrested for armed robbery. He was responsible for a series of robberies of small grocery stores in the area. He was using a gun. Much to Howard's disappointment, but typical of the Juvenile Justice System, the little bastard was back home in six months. Brad was in and out of detention as a juvenile and as an adult for many years. The burglary rate would always rise when he was home.

In 1989, while Howard was supervising the DUI Squad, one member of his crew, John Guich, caught Howard's little criminal neighbor *(then twenty-five years old)* after he had abandoned a car containing thousands of dollars worth of stolen property. Police radio announced that officers were chasing the young man on foot. John drove to the area where he anticipated the thief would run and parked the police car near Ballard High School. When the fleeing man neared, John jumped out of the police car and pursued on foot. The burly officer presented an imposing figure to the swift little burglar. Even though John was a large man, he was pretty good on his feet after several years of serving on the Police K-9 Unit. Brad could have easily outrun John, but he was startled by the sight of the intimidating figure exiting the police car and yelling at him. Brad stumbled and fell as a result of paying more attention to where John was than to where he was running. When John jumped on Brad, the chase was over. This time Brad went away for a long time. John was promoted to the rank of Sergeant a couple of years later. He went on to supervise the DUI Squad for a few years, and then he supervised a patrol squad in the North Precinct until his retirement.

Unfortunately, Howard's neighbor was not the only thief around Ballard. Howard was off duty and preparing to go jogging at Greenlake Park at 9 a.m. one beautiful day in May, 1981. He was dressed in running shorts, tee-shirt, and running shoes *(no gun, no badge, and no ID card)*. All he had taken with him was a driver's license, because he was afraid of having his wallet stolen from his car at the park.

As Howard walked toward his car, he noticed a teenager, who was a stranger to the neighborhood, walking away from a house on the street at the end of the block. Howard drove past him and looked back. The teen crossed the roadway and walked back in the other direction. Strangers reversing their direction of travel are always suspect. He was also staring at the houses as he passed by them. Howard made a left turn at the end of the block, but turned around and parked in a strategic position. He observed the teen *(fictitious name "Stew")* walk to the porch of a neighbor's home and ring the bell. Stew then looked up and down the street. He stood on the porch for about one minute, as he looked into the living room window and knocked on the door. He then walked around the side of the house. One did not need police experience to interpret this kid's body language.

Howard walked to the house next door. The retired university professor who resided there had his front door open, and he was vacuuming. Howard pulled on his vacuum hose to get his attention and asked him to call 911. He knew Howard was a police officer. He told the old professor what had been observed and said that he would watch the residence until on-duty police arrived. Instead of doing what Howard had asked, the man got excited and said, "I'll go this way and you go that way," and he ran around to the rear of the neighbor's house. By the time Howard ran around the other side of the house, the professor had confronted Stew as he was trying to open the back window. The professor asked Stew what he was doing there.

Stew answered, "I'm just cutting through on my way to school." When asked if he knew who lived at that residence, Stew answered that he did not know anyone there.

Howard asked, "Then why did you ring the doorbell and look in the window?" Stew replied that he did not ring the bell or look in the window.

Howard explained to Stew that he was a police officer and that he had watched him ring the doorbell and look in the window of the house. Stew was told he was under arrest, and Howard took a firm grasp of his right wrist. The professor was asked to call 911 and have officers meet Howard at the corner. As Stew was guided across the street, he jerked his arm free and started to run off balance. He fell to the sidewalk. As Howard was overtaking him, he got up and sidestepped as he turned to run in the opposite direction. Howard dove at him, reaching back with his left hand to grab the flailing kid. The force of his momentum caused the determined officer's arm to be torn out of the shoulder socket as he grasped Stew's clothing. Howard managed to fall on top of Stew and was able to keep his weight on the struggling kid. He very painfully rolled over and placed a loose chokehold on Stew's neck, using his right arm. *(This was before cops had been deprived of the use of the neck hold.)* To impress upon Stew that he had no intention of letting him escape, Howard told him, "I'll squeeze your little fucking head right off of your shoulders if you make a move." Even such a proud professional will resort to rude profanity when necessary, to make a point when panic sets in. Howard could not find words to describe the pain in his shoulder caused by the dislocation. His left arm was dangling loosely on the ground. The professor came to his front door and said that the police radio operator had asked if he wanted a "fast back-up." Howard screamed, "I'm hurt! Just tell them to send an aid car and police— Fast!"

Help arrived quickly. Stew was booked into the Youth Center, and Howard was transported to a hospital. He was in so much pain that he was rude and profane to everyone. He begged for pain killers. An inconsiderate nurse said, "I can't give you anything but aspirin until a doctor sees you."

"Anything! Anything!" he responded. After a few minutes that seemed like hours, a doctor came in with a syringe of Demerol. When that wonder-drug had settled in, the pain ceased, and all of Howard's troubles were forgotten.

The doctor approached and said, "We are using a new method of resetting dislocated shoulders called the 'ski-slope technique.'" He continued, "It is a first aid method developed for skiing accidents, and it might seem very crude when I have to put my knee in your ribs for leverage. I will have to wrench on your arm pretty forcibly, but the technique works well— Have any problem with that?"

"No doctor—Anything is better than this!" was Howard's reply. It did look gruesome, but the doctor reinserted Howard's arm back into the shoulder socket.

Howard had to sleep sitting in an inclined, upright position for six weeks because of the pain. It took eighteen months to fully rehabilitate the shoulder. Stew was only charged with two misdemeanors, Criminal Trespass and Resisting Arrest, rather than Attempted Burglary. The rationale for the lesser charges was that he had not completed his entry into the home. Because Stew was a juvenile, he did not have to serve a jail sentence for all the misery he had caused. Howard was outraged to find out that sixteen-year-old Stew had been arrested seven times previously for Burglary. Within a month, word reached Howard that he was continuing to burglarize homes.

The following is an account of a 1992 incident which caused Howard to invest many hours of personal time. The incident also caused him to experience a high level of anxiety. It is an example of how personally involved a cop can become with a career criminal. Howard had been jogging at Greenlake, in Seattle, every other day since 1980. Jogging helped to keep his stress level down. However, the parking lots at Greenlake are areas of a high number of car prowl incidents. Cops instinctively notice suspicious circumstances, even when engaged in recreational activities that are meant to be a pleasant distraction from law enforcement. Howard's recreational trips became another source of stress for him. Here is how he tells the story:

Biography of a Professional Criminal. "The day after Christmas in 1992, I was finishing my tour around the jogging path and observed a tall, thin man, about forty, peering into the windows of a sports utility wagon. My truck was close by, so I sat and watched the suspect, who was later identified as "Calvin." His license plate number was noted and copied as he drove off in a maroon sedan. Calvin drove to the other end of the lake, where he parked next to a van. He got out and looked in the van windows, hopped back into his maroon sedan and moved to a third lot. By this time, he noticed that he was being watched, and quickly left the scene. Thieves of this caliber seem to have a sixth sense—seeming to know when someone is observing their actions. I was upset that I had not yet purchased a cell phone, and there were no pay phones available as my surveillance of Calvin continued. A patrol officer happened by, and he was given the information relating to Calvin's activities and his car. The registration check on the car that Calvin was driving showed a report of sale, and the title had not been changed.

"Two days later, one of the early watch officers told me of a car prowl report he had taken that morning at Greenlake. A witness had observed a suspect matching Calvin's description driving a maroon sedan with the same license plate. A report was submitted to the detectives that related my observations two days prior to the car prowling incident.

"Another computer check for the registration of the maroon sedan was made a week later. Just as a law-abiding citizen should, Calvin had changed the title of the car to his name. It was determined from computer information that Calvin was being investigated for fourteen forgery incidents and two credit card frauds in 1989, 1990, and 1992. That is what many good car prowlers do. They steal cash, checkbooks and credit cards, and they also commit forgeries. I checked a mug shot of Calvin from our Identification Bureau and confirmed that the active big guy at Greenlake was Calvin. Now the detectives would be able to get a warrant for every case in which a witness could identify Calvin from a photomontage.

"I continued to check for warrants on Calvin on a regular basis, because I saw him at the lake at least once a month; but I never was able to catch him in the act. We were getting plenty of car prowl reports, and Calvin matched many of the descriptions of the ones for which we were lucky enough to have a witness.

"Finally, in August 1993, I saw old Calvin approaching a black VW convertible, just as if he owned it. Knowing how alert he was, I jogged down the path and doubled back along the lakeshore. Inserting myself into a large bush, I watched Calvin go through his act. My heart was pounding so hard that I was afraid he might hear it. It also occurred to me that someone walking along the pathway might call 911 and report me as an old pervert hiding in the bushes. There are plenty of those at Greenlake too. Calvin had opened the trunk of the VW and was looking around inside. When someone walked by, he would act as if he were doing his stretching exercises in back of his own car. On one occasion, he even slipped off his shirt and threw it in the trunk, closed the trunk lid easily, and started to walk away. As soon as the passer-by was gone, Calvin came right back to the trunk. I didn't jump on him then, because I thought he might have purchased another car, and I would look pretty stupid jumping on him if it turned out to be his own car. I had not seen his old maroon car in the parking lot. He took his shirt out of the trunk and started walking away. Then I caught sight of the maroon sedan, but it was too late. Calvin spotted me and hurriedly entered his car as I was running at him and yelling his name. He was having a very bad day, as he had found nothing of value to steal after going through a lengthy routine; and then a crazy gray-haired old man chased him out of the park.

"I was angry at myself for not acting more quickly; but now there was probable cause for Calvin's arrest, which had been so difficult to obtain during the previous eight months. Even though he didn't steal anything, there was still a strong vehicle prowling charge. Calvin was finally arrested in September, and he was identified and charged in several other theft incidents. The wait to testify against Calvin in court lasted for months, as his public defender kept finding excuses for continuances. This is a tactic that defense attorneys use on occasion, to discourage civilian witnesses. Witnesses get tired of coming to court and being told that they are not needed, and that they will have to come back on another day. One can only afford to miss so much work for such a purpose. Then, in January 1994, I was contacted by a deputy prosecuting attorney who told me that my charge against Calvin had been disposed of. He told me that because Calvin had so many other charges pending, including felony investigations, that he had my case "stricken" *(thrown out)* because nothing was taken from the trunk. I explained, in a strained voice, how I had invested more than eight months of my life to catch this guy. The prosecutor apologized. Calvin and his public defender somehow managed to have three other charges dismissed also.

"On January 24, 1994, an early watch officer forwarded another car prowl report from Greenlake, with a suspect description provided by witnesses that matched "you know who" driving a maroon sedan. In February 1994, while I was jogging, Calvin showed up at Greenlake in a Cadillac driven by his female friend. When he saw me, he ran from the car. I introduced myself to his female friend by showing her my police identity card and took her identification with me as I ran after Calvin on the pathway. It is hard to imagine what other park users were thinking, seeing the gray-haired old guy running and screaming at a 6-foot-2-inch man that he was going to have to talk to me then, or talk to me later. He could have kicked my butt in a minute. I finally gave up and returned to talk to the woman in the Cadillac. She allowed me to search her car. Nothing was found except for a screwdriver that Calvin had thrown under the car. A police unit finally responded, and a citation was written to the female friend for driving with a suspended driver's license, and for not having insurance. Calvin came back to see what was happening to his friend. I told Calvin that I was the one who had been watching him for the past year, and that I was taking his crimes at Greenlake personally. He was invited to never come back, and he has not been seen at the lake since. He may have won in the courtroom, but my favorite city park was safe from the wrath of this predator.

"On May 16, 1994, Calvin bought a used car and left his maroon sedan at the dealer lot. When the dealer moved Calvin's old car, he found checks under the seat that had been stolen in a car prowl incident. SURPRISE! SURPRISE!!

"While researching my old files in preparation for writing this story, a "Charge Order" was found relating to one of my 1984 arrests. The charges of Possession of Stolen Property and Felony Vehicle Prowl had been requested by one of our detectives. The suspect mentioned in the report was named "Terry." Then I noticed the small print on the order indicating the suspect's true name, "Calvin." It was surprising to find that I had arrested Calvin in1984 for burglary of a motor home *(Felony Vehicle Prowl)*, taking a television set, and driving a stolen VW. Coincidentally, the VW had been stolen from the Greenlake area two days earlier.

"This forgotten incident occurred while I was assigned to police motorcycles and working a Sea Hawks football game at the Kingdome. There had been a significant car prowl problem during Kingdome events that drew the attention of a television news team. They attended our roll call. The news team rode in one of our traffic cars, and my sergeant requested that they were to be called to the scene of any arrests. This was interpreted as a personal challenge; and after the crowd was in the dome, I positioned myself under Interstate 5, where I could observe about four square blocks of parked cars. It was not long before a male was seen driving suspiciously around the quiet parking lots in a VW Bug. *(It turned out to be Calvin.)* He stopped by a motor home, walked around it, and then broke the door open. Back-up units and the news team were immediately requested to respond. I surprised Calvin when he was walking to the VW with a television in his arms. He had nowhere to run, and I was the star of television news on that Sunday evening. Of course, Calvin offered one of his many aliases, and that is why I didn't remember him when I contacted him regarding the 1993 car prowls.

"Checking back to see how the justice system had handled Calvin for the 1984 auto theft and motor home burglary, I found that the auto theft was not charged, but Calvin was charged and convicted of a number of charges that included charges from my arrest. He received a sentence of fifteen years with ten years suspended for Felony Vehicle Prowl, Possession of Stolen Property, Burglary, and First Degree Theft. Calvin went to prison in January 1985, and he was paroled in March 1987. What had our hero been up to since he was given another chance? In October 1987, he was arrested for shoplifting. In July 1988, he was arrested on a warrant for failing to appear in court on the shoplifting charge and for False Reporting *(giving a false name to the officer)*. He was convicted and sentenced to 180 days with 175 days suspended. He had to serve five whole days. On July 24, 1989, Calvin was arrested on two counts of forgery and one count of first-degree theft. Failing to show for court on these charges, he was arrested at least once again on warrants before he was finally convicted and sentenced to 36 months. He was sent to prison in February 1990. On May 16, 1990, after serving less than four months of his three-year sentence, Calvin was arrested on a warrant for Felony Theft from a 1989 incident. He was convicted in June 1990 and sentenced to two years. In March 1992, Calvin was on the loose again. He was arrested for Escape, Drug Possession, and False Reporting. These charges were dismissed for some unknown reason. Someone must have thought that Calvin needed a break. He must have been sent back to the prison from where he escaped, because no one heard from him until I started seeing him around Greenlake in December of 1992. He stayed busy around Greenlake and in court in 1993. The system finally caught up with Calvin in August 1994 when he was arrested, charged, and convicted of Residential Burglary. He was sentenced to 63 months and entered prison in December1994. YES!!

"One might think that at last there was finally some justice. Not really! Let the reader decide the quality of the justice system, after considering how the system had allowed Calvin to victimize an untold number of innocent persons, even before I met him back in 1984. When he turned eighteen in 1969, he was arrested for larceny and robbery, but he was not charged. One can only speculate that the robbery may have been drug related, because those incidents are not prosecuted on many occasions. Also, in 1969 he was convicted of burglary and served one month, with three years probation. In 1970, Calvin was arrested for assault and burglary, but not charged. In 1971, a robbery was dismissed. In September 1972, Calvin was convicted of grand larceny and sentenced to seven and one-half years with seven years suspended. He didn't wait long after being released to get himself convicted of burglary and attempted grand larceny in April of 1973. He received a fifteen-year sentence and was released on parole on September 25, 1975. After serving over two years in prison, Calvin still "didn't get it." He was arrested for auto theft in July 1976. He was not charged for that incident, probably because his parole was revoked, and he had to go back and serve a little more time. In 1977, Calvin was arrested for escape, promoting prostitution, and a probation violation. Then warrants started piling up, and he moved to Portland for awhile. He was arrested there in November 1981, and sent back with warrants for two counts of forgery and two counts of "Fugitive from Justice." One count of forgery was dismissed, and he was convicted of one forgery count. He was sentenced to sixty days in jail and five years probation. On November 10, 1982, Calvin was arrested for possession of stolen property. He must have stayed in hiding or traveled out of state again because he was not sentenced on the 1981 possession of stolen property until he appeared on the charges that I had arrested him for at the Kingdome on December 2, 1984.

"Losing my charges on Calvin in 1993, after chasing him for over a year, does not seem nearly as bad after finding out just how Calvin has ripped off the justice system—over 37 arrests, mostly felonies, from the time he was eighteen until he reached age forty-three. During that twenty-five-year period, Calvin served a grand total of approximately six and one-half years in custody. The other eighteen and one-half years were spent committing crimes on a daily basis. I cannot say that justice has been served now that the system has finally done something with Calvin, when I think of the free pass he was given for twenty-five years. Consider the many hundreds of people who have been the victims of crimes committed by Calvin for which he was not apprehended."

Recreational trips to Greenlake would never be the same. Howard would see many more car prowlers, and he would be responsible for catching several of them. One such incident occurred not long after he last observed Calvin at the lake in 1993. He was following a thief whom he had watched steal a purse from the trunk of a car. When the suspect noticed that a truck was following his car, he panicked and stopped. The suspect exited his car in an attempt to intimidate the old guy in the truck. Howard jumped out and identified himself, and told the guy to get against his car. The suspect dove into his open door and started to drive off as Howard was holding his arm with one hand, and pepper-spraying him with his free hand. After being dragged a few feet, Howard was forced to let go. The license number of the suspect's car was registered to a woman in the South End who said her son, Joe Patterson, drove the car. She said Joe was living in a motel on Aurora Avenue North. *(Highway 99)* Howard's patrol squad found the suspect in a motel on Aurora Avenue later in the day while he was on duty. The officers called Howard to the motel. When they asked the thief's girlfriend if he acted strangely when he arrived home on that morning, she said that Joe did not say anything to her—he just went straight to the bathroom and washed his face for a long while. Upon searching Joe's car, officers recovered two expensive tennis rackets and other items that were reported stolen at Greenlake that morning. The items came from a car owned by a Seattle Firefighter.

By 1996, Howard was still enjoying his law enforcement duties, but he could feel retirement getting close. This fact did not cause him to back off from any dangerous circumstance. His next near-death experience *(his ninth)* would be the most exciting and disturbing.

CHAPTER 11

The Bank Robber Known as Hollywood

Over a period of four years *(1992-1996)*, a strikingly good-looking man in his late 30s to early 40s had committed sixteen bank robberies—fourteen in Seattle, and two in Portland. Upon committing the seventeenth robbery, this man, whose name was discovered to be William Scott Scurlock *(preferred name, Scott)* provided the ninth near-death experience for Howard. The fact that Scott had been able to rob sixteen banks, leaving the FBI without a clue to his identity, not to mention the fact that his profit from the robberies far exceeded that of the average bank robber, is evidence of his meticulous planning. To say the robberies were "well-planned" is an understatement.

Burdena Pasenelli, then Special Agent in Charge For FBI Operations in Washington State *(coincidentally, Howard's former Seattle Police Academy classmate)*, stated that Scurlock was considered to have taken more money in his seventeen bank robberies than any one Los Angeles bank robber had ever taken to date. Los Angeles was considered a "Mecca" for bank robbers. The FBI tagged Scott with the nickname "Hollywood" because of his use of heavy pancake makeup, wigs, false mustaches, and prosthetics that changed his facial features.

Scott grew up in Reston, Virginia. Although he was the son of a preacher, he was known to be a wild kid—an adventure seeker. That would be something that he would have in common with Howard. The difference between them is that Scott expanded his practice of risking life and limb to committing thefts and dealing drugs. Scott joined a friend who was going to college in Hawaii in the mid-seventies. He worked on farms while in Hawaii to support himself. After stumbling upon someone's marijuana plants in the fields, he began stealing from the crop. It was not long before he was growing his own on the farm where he worked. In the late 70s, Scott returned to the mainland and settled in at Evergreen State College, near Olympia, Washington. He began producing crystal meth in the school lab and became a successful entrepreneur in the drug trade. He supported himself and his associates in grand style on the proceeds from the drug sales. Avoiding contact with the criminal justice system until that fateful seventeenth bank robbery was indicative of his high level of intelligence.

In the early 1980s, Scott rented a wooded, nine-acre site in a rural setting near Olympia, Washington. The property contained an old house, a barn, an outbuilding, and a tree house. Scott preferred living in the tree house, and he sublet the house and outbuilding. He eventually purchased the property and remodeled the tree house and other buildings, using the big bucks that he earned from selling crystal meth.

In 1986, The Seattle Times newspaper published a large pictorial review of the unique living quarters of William Scott Scurlock. The newspaper published photographs of the inside and outside of the tree house. One photograph showed Scott sitting in a living-room chair. With close scrutiny, one could see a wide-brimmed hat hanging on a wall that would later appear in bank surveillance photographs published in newspapers. The tale of Scott Scurlock and friends is a story in itself. Famed mystery writer Ann Rule has researched the lives, loves, and adventures of Scott and his closest associates, in her fascinating novel, *The End of the Dream (1999, Pocket Books)*.

The dawn of November 27, 1996, was ushered in by the gray skies and ever-present rain that so defines Seattle in the late autumn. On the late afternoon of this day before Thanksgiving, Hollywood and two skilled accomplices robbed a bank in North Seattle. The FBI Violent Crimes Task Force had been anticipating this hit, and so had many Seattle banks. Hollywood was recognized as soon as he entered the bank, and a silent alarm was immediately activated. While law enforcement units were responding, Hollywood and accomplices Steve Meyers and Mark Biggins were withdrawing $1.08 million from the bank in the Lake City area of Seattle. A Task Force detective, Mike Magan, quickly found and followed the getaway van, and called for a backup. Fortunately, many officers arrived quickly to assist. When the van stopped on a residential side street, Mark and Steve came out shooting. Howard was the sergeant in charge of the patrol squad involved in backing up the detective. He was taking one of his delayed furlough days off and had appointed an acting sergeant, Officer Jack Napolitano, to supervise the squad for that day. A friend in the police communications unit knew that Howard would want to know if members of his squad were in trouble, and alerted him by telephone.

As one officer from the squad arrived at the scene, the windshield of his patrol car exploded into icy shards of glass, as shots rang forth. Another officer later spoke of hearing bullets whistle passed his ears. Fortunately for officers and FBI agents, one of the robbers' automatic weapons had jammed. Then Mark and Steve jumped back in the van, and Scott drove off again. They stopped several times to continue firing at officers. Both accomplices were struck by return fire and captured. Hollywood ran off into a dark residential area.

Howard had been listening to his portable police radio at home, and he was making phone calls attempting to obtain authorization to join his squad. He was told that there were plenty of supervisors available. The search for Hollywood went on for hours. Police dogs scoured the entire area. Police units were answering call after call from residents who believed that someone was hiding in their garage, back porch, or wood shed. All suspicious circumstance calls were checked, to no avail. The search was finally called off for the night. Plain clothes units and patrol cars were assigned to the area until the next morning.

Howard reported for duty on Thanksgiving Day, and had roll call for the squad at 11:30 a.m. The topic of the day was the big shootout. Several officers who had fired their weapons had to be placed on administrative duties, as is the policy in all shooting incidents. Everyone believed that Hollywood had once again outsmarted the cops, and that he had slipped away in the darkness.

At 2:36 p.m., two units received a call to check on a possible prowler in a back yard of a residence that is just blocks from where Hollywood had disappeared. The caller was still concerned about the manhunt from the previous evening and thought he had seen movement inside a 10-foot camper that was stored on blocks in the yard. Howard decided to respond with the officers, even though it was unlikely that Hollywood was still in the area, in light of the intense search that had already been conducted.

The resident met officers at the sidewalk and showed them the best approach to the camper to prevent an escape if someone were inside. Howard asked the resident if he was positive that he had seen someone in the camper. He said that he was not positive, but he thought he had seen the curtain move. He told Howard that there had been trouble with kids entering the camper in the past. Other officers arrived, and the group carefully approached the camper from different directions. A cable lock secured the main doorway to the camper. Curtains on the side windows were drawn shut. The window on the north end of the camper had an object resembling a furniture cushion pushed against it. Howard knocked on the east window and the door to the camper, and yelled, "Seattle Police." Even though he thought that there was no one in the camper, he was still careful in positioning himself to the side of the door and window just in case. One of the officers again announced police presence and ordered anyone inside to come out. There was no response and no movement from inside. The resident was asked to remove the cable lock from the door, but the door was also locked from the inside. He had misplaced the door key. Officers were shown a trap door, approximately twelve inches high by eighteen inches wide. It was on the lower west side, and seemed to be blocked shut by something inside the camper. One officer was able to shine his flashlight into a small upper window on the north side, and he saw no person or movement inside. They did not want to leave until they determined if someone was inside or not; so the sergeant emptied two canisters of pepper spray into a partially open window. It is difficult to imagine someone surviving in that confined space without screaming, or at least coughing from the effects of the oleoresin capsicum spray. All of the officers were convinced that there was probably no one in the camper and that it was safe enough to break in.

Howard gave the order for officers to take cover. Officer Jon Dittoe covered the sergeant as he used a four-foot board to break the lock on a slider window on the north side. He reached over and pulled the window fully open and waited for a few seconds to see if there would be a reaction, then pushed the cushion away that was blocking the window from inside. As he prepared to carefully shine a flashlight inside, an ear-shattering gunshot rang out from the camper. Howard radioed that shots had been fired as he ran for cover, hearing multiple gunshots behind him. A student officer already occupied the closest tree, and Howard couldn't get close enough to the tree trunk to keep from being exposed to gunfire. He didn't think it would be quite fair to "pull rank" on the kid and kick him out of there, so he broke and ran for the next tree. Rapid semi-automatic gunfire rang out again, and he hit the ground and started crawling fast. The curtains in the camper window were moving, and he was certain he was about to be killed. In fact, there had been no opportunity to check himself for wounds after the first gunshot. Once Howard was safely behind a large tree about forty feet from the camper, he heard Officer Dittoe yell for cover fire so that he could move to a safer location. Howard fired several rounds from his 357-Magnum revolver at the west window of the camper, and two other officers fired about ten rounds each from their 9-mm semi-automatics. This allowed Dittoe to retreat about thirty feet to a large fir tree.

Next, a barrage of cover fire was used to protect the student officer as he retreated to a more secure position. They were now a little safer, but still pinned down in the large yard awaiting rescue. Their greatest concern was that Hollywood would become desperate and charge out of the camper in a blaze of semi-automatic weapon fire. They had used most of their ammunition, and Officer Dittoe had used both of his clips. More ammunition clips were called for. Assistance from a television station helicopter was also requested to watch for an attempted escape into the yard to the east. It had seemed impossible that anyone might exit from the east window; but after what they had just experienced, the officers thought anything was possible.

Finally, help started to arrive. The student officer was able to leave the yard, and he returned with a shotgun in hand. Howard told him to train the shotgun on the camper door and gave him instructions to fire immediately if Hollywood exited with a firearm in hand, or tried to escape. The possibility of Hollywood surprising and killing one or more of the officers who were assisting with traffic control and containing the perimeter needed to be eliminated. They were pinned down in the yard for about 45 minutes before the Emergency Response Team officers covered them and took the officers out of the yard one by one.

By this time, Howard and his crew were physically and emotionally drained. They were still plagued by three concerns: First, someone could be killed by Hollywood before he was captured; Second, somehow he might have escaped while they were scrambling to safety; Third, the question of how an officer would survive the mental trauma after finding out if one of his bullets had killed Hollywood.

Howard was suffering great pain in his right hand, which was bleeding and blistered from what turned out to be a burn caused by flame expelled from the cylinder of his gun. He had been so frozen with fear that he didn't even feel the burn when it happened. The Emergency Response Team and the Hostage Negotiation Team worked for several hours to coax Hollywood from the camper. They finally made their forced entry using tear gas and stun grenades. What they found was Hollywood's body wedged under blankets. He had about seven or eight bullet holes in him. That information magnified the concern of the officers. About seventy bullet holes were found in the walls and windows of the camper. All of those who had fired upon the camper were both relieved and embarrassed when the Medical Examiner's office came out with a report that Hollywood had fired one shot, and that was a shot to his head that had killed him. What that meant is that they had fired about seventy rounds at a dead man. Howard took a little kidding by some peers who were amused that they had fired so many rounds and that the sergeant had made a call for more ammunition.

The many rounds of semi-automatic gunfire that Howard had heard while running for cover were from Officer Dittoe, who had been covering him. Dittoe had emptied a 15-round clip after Hollywood fired his first and only shot. He then reloaded and emptied another 15-round clip to provide cover for himself, as he ran for the tree that was occupied by the student officer. Those thirty rounds were appropriate and necessary; but they were what caused all involved to believe that a small war was going on. Officer Dittoe had performed his duty to provide cover for his sergeant in an exceptional manner, and Howard will be eternally grateful for that.

Officers worked many hours of overtime on that Thanksgiving Day. Turkey dinners were cold. The old sergeant did not sleep well that night. He woke up in the early morning hours, dreaming that he was being fired upon. He screamed to Liz, "Get on the floor—They are shooting at us!" Nightmares persisted for the next week. Things got a little better as the days passed.

By some miracle, all officers came through this event without serious physical injury; however, most retain some degree of emotional scarring. The Seattle Police Department Psychologist, Dr. Mar, organized a psychological debriefing, which included all FBI agents and police officers involved in the two-day event. During the debriefing, the stress and emotional strife were evident in the voices and on the faces of participants. Also evident was the relief that participants experienced as a result of this carefully orchestrated session. It was a healing experience to share feelings, and to find that officers involved in both the shooting the night before, and the Thanksgiving Day shooting, had suffered similar adverse effects. Howard held a firm belief that the psychological debriefings he had participated in during his career played an important roll in the maintenance of his mental health, and thus his professional success.

Now all that they had to worry about were the results of the Shooting Review Board. Even though they were personally aware of terrible misjudgments by the board in the past, they knew their shooting would be justified. They would only have to defend the great number of shots fired. The shooting review went well. The board members looked very closely at the issue of cover fire, because cover fire had never been a part of the firearms training. It will probably be included in the future.

Hollywood provided the ninth "near-death experience" that Howard had encountered during his career. What Howard was most thankful for was that Hollywood didn't kill him when he had a great opportunity to do so. The sergeant was eternally grateful to William Scott Scurlock for that. No doubt, he was a prolific bank robber—but he was not a killer!

As for Mark Biggens and Steve Meyers—they were attempting to kill officers to facilitate a getaway on the previous evening. Their wounds healed, and they pled guilty to bank robbery and assault charges. They did this to avoid a prison sentence that would have placed them in prison and kept them incarcerated until they were elderly. For their plea bargain, they each received a sentence of twenty-one years in a federal prison.

CHAPTER 12

The End

Twenty-nine years of giving one hundred percent to the law enforcement profession had taken its toll, physically and emotionally. In 1994, a problem with irregular heartbeat caused Howard to seek a specialist at the age of fifty-six. The diagnosis was that Howard had a defective heart valve. Blood was leaking back through the aortic valve, causing the heart chamber to become enlarged. The condition was stabilized with medication, and he continued to work at his same energetic level for another three years—retiring in 1997. Retirement was not something that Howard had looked forward to, because he so loved his profession.

The reality was that he had no choice in the matter. His body was worn out. His attempts to continue the pace of a young man were exhausting, and his old injuries were causing pain that fluctuated from nagging discomfort to torturous agony. Six years after his heart-valve diagnosis, and three years after retirement, Howard still had his original valve that the heart specialist had told him would probably have to be replaced in five years. That was good, but the wear and tear to his hands, shoulders, and back that were the results of injuries he had suffered caused him to feel like a man in his eighties. His vertigo still hampered his balance, and the pills he had been taking for six years drained his energy.

Howard accepted retirement gracefully. It was an opportunity to dedicate himself full time to a book project that he had begun fifteen years earlier. He had received scores of rejections from book publishers over the years, but he was finally able to produce a product that was acceptable to one publisher who had faith in Howard's work. A lifelong dream was accomplished when his law enforcement textbook was published. *(How Police Officers Get Hired/The Key to Getting the Cop Job And Keeping It, 1999, The Graduate Group)*

As a young man, Howard would tell his friends and associates that he would not survive beyond age fifty because of the fast pace of his life. He was nearly ten years beyond his life expectation, and he was satisfied with his accomplishments. He thought that it was time to relax and enjoy retirement. This was easier said than done. Even though he attempted to take life easy, whatever that old nemesis was that had caused criminals to find Howard did not go away. He tried not to be a cop, but it was difficult to ignore the obvious—like the time Liz heard a noise outside in the middle of the night and awakened Howard. He slipped on his trousers and shower shoes, grabbed his cell phone, and ended up following a thief for ten minutes until officers arrived in the area. Howard continued to see car prowlers on his jogging trips to Greenlake Park. One such event was unusually difficult. Howard provided the following written statement for a Burglary/Theft Unit Detective:

SUBJECT: SPD INCIDENT # 97-496796 THEFT/ CARPROWL 11-15-97 Just after 0900 hours on Saturday, November 15, 1997, I had just finished jogging at Greenlake Park. I was returning to my truck, which was parked in a lot across from the Aqua Theater in the 5700 block of W. Greenlake Dr. North—just west of the tennis courts, when I saw a black male, 40 to 50 years-of-age, 6 ft plus, and having one to two weeks' growth of salt and pepper beard. The man had walked through the parking lot past the rear of my truck. I do not recall his clothing other than he was not wearing clothing that would normally be used for jogging. I was focusing my attention on his face to determine if he was the infamous "Calvin," a car prowler I had observed at Greenlake on several occasions.

I entered my truck and began to back out of my parking place, but had to wait as the male I had observed was driving through the lot in back of me. He was driving a late 70s or early 80s Chevrolet—dull silver or gray in color. The rear window was gone and covered by plastic. I pulled out of the lot to Greenlake Drive behind the Chevrolet. I noticed that the man turned into the tennis court parking lot and drove slowly the length of the long lot and back. I had parked to watch. He reentered Greenlake Drive, and then entered the parking lots adjacent to the soccer fields. Within 100 feet, he pulled into an angle parking space between other cars. He sat there for a few minutes as several people were milling around that area. He then backed out and continued southbound in the soccer field lot to the 5200 block of Greenlake Way, N., and pulled into another angle parking space—to the left of a large black truck. The truck had a license something like "A32886"? I drove past and tried to scribble the license number of the Chevrolet. I checked what I had written later when I contacted 911, but it was difficult to read. It was something like "EYF 387."

As I drove past, the male had exited his vehicle and was walking past the back of the black truck. I saw the male disappear between the parked cars and I turned around. He was nowhere to be seen. I had only lost sight of him for about 30 seconds. I turned around again and stopped near the back of the black truck, and I saw the male through the right side mirror of the truck as he was moving around in the right front seat. As I was dialing 911 on my cell phone, he exited the black truck and went back to the Chevrolet. He started backing out of the parking space very fast, nearly striking a car that was N/B in the parking lot. He ran the stop sign entering Greenlake way, made a left turn to N. 52nd St, and made several turns as he zigzagged through residential streets. I lost sight of the Chevrolet when he ran a red light at estimated 30-mph S/B on Wallingford Av. N. at N. 50th St. Cross traffic had to slow to avoid an accident. I returned to the black truck and found an embarrassed victim nearby. Officer Doug Brown arrived, and I described what I had observed. I overheard the owner of the black truck tell Officer Brown that $265 in cash and his hunting license had been removed from a wallet that was in the truck. The victim also stated that when he parked the truck he had locked the truck doors with the electric lock. He said both doors were locked. After the thief exited the truck, the passenger side door was unlocked and the driver's side was still locked. I looked closely and I could see no damage to the passenger side door or door lock.

On Friday, November 21, 1997, Detective Larson asked me to read admonishments concerning witnesses observing photomontages. It indicated that I would be shown a montage of photos that might or might not contain a photograph of the person I had observed prowling the black truck. After observing several cards of booking photographs, I was able to identify the person whom I had seen driving the gray Chevrolet, and who had entered the victim's black truck on November 15, 1997 at Greenlake Park.

To the astonishment of Howard and Officer Brown, the jogger *(victim)* was a former police officer from the East Coast. It was no wonder that the victim was upset about having provided such an easy opportunity for a crook.

The detective filed charges, and Howard was required to appear in court six months later, when the guy was picked up on a warrant. The witnesses showed for the trial, including the victim who had lost his wallet. As is common when all witnesses are present, the defense lawyer knew he didn't have a chance, so the thief entered a guilty plea. His criminal record was so bad that the judge sentenced him to a year in jail—ninety days to serve, and the remainder of the jail time suspended on the condition of no further criminal offenses. Upon completion of his time served, the judge ordered him turned over to Snohomish County for a theft warrant in that jurisdiction. That had everyone in the courtroom doing high-fives.

Greenlake Park was the one place that Howard had counted on for stress relief, but car prowlers had ruined that diversion for him. Other sources of stress in his retirement were the continuing reminders of repulsive and/or horrifying experiences.

No matter what area of the city he traveled, he could not drive one mile without reliving a circumstance wherein someone suffered an unnatural end to their life, or was victimized in some traumatic way. One of Howard's personal traits was his empathy for victims of crimes, and he could not escape those feelings after retirement.

He did not enjoy being reminded of the elderly Alzheimer's disease sufferer who was left to die from malnutrition and exposure in a basement room of a state-licensed care home. The brother of the woman who owned the facility, a five-bedroom house, told Howard that the woman had been moved to the basement because she annoyed his sister. When he would ask his sister if she wanted him to take meals downstairs to the elderly woman, his sister would say, "If she can't get herself up here to eat at the table with the rest of us, then she can do without." He told Howard that the woman had been without food for ten days. It was December, and the weather had been near freezing, or below. There was no heat in the room, and a window was open for the woman's dog to get in and out for dog food that was left on the back porch. Every time Howard drives near the Lake City area of Seattle, the vision of that poor emaciated old woman in the freezing basement room wounds his heart. What adds to the inhumanity is the fact that the owner of the home was not charged. At that time, Homicide by Neglect was considered a difficult charge to prove in court; but if there ever was a case where all of the elements of the crime were present, that was the case.

Another Lake City tragedy that continued to cause great distress for the retired old sergeant was an accident investigation wherein a seven-year-old boy was crushed by a metro bus. The youngster was visiting his grandparents. They were getting ready to take him to his favorite fast-food restaurant when he begged them to let him take his new bicycle for a quick ride. They relented, and within minutes he had busted through a stop sign, crossing an arterial street directly into the path of the large bus. Much to Howard's dismay, he had to contain the accident scene for hours so that the Accident Investigation Unit detectives could complete their investigation. Howard wanted to have the little bleeding body transported away, but the investigators were adamant about keeping the scene intact. The police department psychologist held a debriefing for everyone involved in the incident, including the bus driver and his supervisors, patrol officers, parking enforcement officers, and investigators. The trauma expressed by every person at the debriefing was similar. Everyone carried a deep emotional burden as a result of their firsthand involvement in the tragedy.

A South End example of Howard's troubling memories is one of a domestic violence incident, which progressed to a catastrophe. A young woman had separated from her 25-year-old husband because of his severe mental problems. The woman was temporarily living with her parents. Cops responded to a police radio call when the troubled husband went to the parents' home while his wife was there alone. The young woman saw his car arrive and called the police right away. When the woman refused to admit the man to the house, he punched out a back-door window and forced his way into the home. He twisted his wife's arm in back of her. She managed to break free and locked herself and their baby in a bedroom. She told the husband that the police were on the way, and he left the house. From a description of his car, broadcast by radio, Howard was able to stop the young husband about a mile from the parents' home. The suspect was bleeding very badly from a large gash in his forehead, caused by the broken glass in the back door. He was emotionally unstable, so Howard humored him into being cooperative until backup units arrived. Experience had taught him that physical violence can occasionally be avoided by listening attentively, and then showing empathy and compassion. This is a technique exceedingly more acceptable than the pain and complaints that come with the use of physical force.

The distraught young man poured out his marital troubles, and he told Howard of his bitterness over his wife and baby abandoning him. In a very serious tone of voice, the man said, "As soon as I am released from jail, I'm going to kill her." Howard told him that he must love his wife and child and couldn't possibly be serious about what he was saying. With a determined look on his face he said, "I mean it. She's a dead woman."

Backup units arrived. Because of the serious threats and violence that had occurred at the house, the arrest was processed very cautiously. They charged the man with Property Damage, Criminal Trespass, Assault, and Menacing With Threats to Kill, and requested that he not be allowed to bail out of jail until a judge could review the case. Naturally, the man was convicted of all of the misdemeanor charges. *(NOTE -This crime occurred prior to when the crime of "Threats to Kill" was elevated to a felony crime.)* A relatively short jail sentence was imposed, along with some mental counseling. Howard heard no more from the family, and the matter was forgotten. What Howard didn't know was that in their fear for the safety of their daughter, the woman's parents sent her to live in secrecy with a relative, 150 miles from home. The young man learned the address of the home where his wife was hiding by stealing mail at her parents' home. He loaded his car with supplies that included blindfolds, twine, and knives. He drove to the town in southern Washington and parked one block from the house where his wife was staying. He watched until he thought she was home alone and broke into the house. He attempted to abduct his wife by knifepoint, but she resisted. Her screams attracted the attention of a person in another part of the house. As that person was coming to her aid, the husband stabbed his nineteen-year-old wife to death and fled. Howard was sickened by this story, when he was given the details by the prosecuting attorney. His testimony was needed in the murder trial to show premeditation on the part of the killer. Howard kept asking himself why lawmakers cannot create legislation that that would serve to avoid such tragedies when there are strong indications that they are likely to occur. This was just one more of the countless abhorrent memories suffered when Howard traveled the streets of Seattle.

Moving out of Seattle to a suburb afforded some relief. At least the reminders of past trauma were reduced in number; but he was not able to fully abandon his feelings of responsibility for the welfare of others, and the suspicion that if something bad could possibly happen, it would most likely occur in his presence.

On a typical spring day in Western Washington, with a slight breeze blowing scattered, puffy, white clouds through the quiet suburb that he now called home, Howard found some handyman type of errands to run. There were materials to pick up at a local hardware store, for minor repair to their new condominium apartment. After throwing on his grubby jeans and Bald-Eagle sweatshirt, he kissed his wife goodbye; and as Liz was locking the door behind him, he yelled for her to let him back in. It had become a routine for Howard to go out the door and turn right around to retrieve his gun and cell phone. There was still the strong feeling that becoming a victim would not be acceptable, even though there was no longer a requirement to carry the gun. He had also forgotten to take a medical insurance refund check that he wanted to cash. Once the forgotten items were gathered, he kissed Liz again, and said, "OK, I've got everything now. You can lock me out."

She replied in a sarcastic, but kidding tone, "I've heard that before. You'll be back." He laughed and continued on his way. Howard was worried about how forgetful he was becoming. The old head injury was not the cause. He attributed his current confused state to encroaching old age.

First stop was the bank, to cash his check. The bank was busy for early afternoon. Only two of the four tellers' cages were open. A total of five customers were in the two lines. Howard nodded to the loan officer and assistant manager. The two women were seated at their desks at the far end of the single, large, open room. Because of the courteous service they extended to Howard and his wife when they moved to the area, he considered them friends. Howard walked to the shorter of the two lines. He was in no hurry. After all, he was retired, and he had a very flexible schedule. As usual, Howard evaluated every customer in the bank. This is a law enforcement habit that he could never break. The man who was first in line ahead of him was obviously a middle-aged laborer. His work clothes and hands were soiled, and he needed a shave. The woman next in line was a young, stay-at-home mom. The biggest clues were that she was very pregnant, and she had a little boy about four years old in tow. The first two people in the other line, a man and

woman, appeared to be white-collar workers. They were im-
maculately groomed, and were wearing expensive business suits.
The third person in that line was what Howard would consider
a throwback from the 60s—a kid about nineteen, wearing old
blue jeans, a ripped, rock-and-roll tee-shirt, long, purple hair,
and an earring in his nose and eyebrows.

The line had not yet moved when Howard noticed three
male figures approaching the front doors. They were moving
slowly and looking around. Body language was one of Howard's
specialties, and these guys captured his undivided attention
and suspicion. As they entered the bank, one man stayed by the
doors, and the other two split up. They wore black stocking caps
pulled low on their foreheads, and those popular football side-
line jackets. *This is it!* Howard thought. He left the line in an
attempt to put some distance between himself and the tellers.
The stocking caps were actually rolled up ski masks, which were
now pulled down over their faces.

Instinctively, Howard went into the "dissociative response"
that he had developed as a result of innumerable perilous duties. Howard perceived the actions of every person in the bank
as being in slow motion. As before, it seemed as if he were watching the events from outside of his body. The terror on the faces
of the tellers and bank officers was painful to witness. The customers in line had no idea what was occurring until they heard
a gruff bark, "Everybody on the floor— NOW!" A sawed-off,
double-barreled shotgun had been removed from the coat of the
robber closest to the assistant manager; and a revolver was in
the grasp of the other man by the teller cages. The robber at the
door had turned around, and was looking out toward the parking lot.

Howard knew he would not be able to fish his 9-mm pistol
out of his fanny pack while he remained standing. If he would
not have complied and placed himself on the floor, they would
have opened up on him. He moved slowly into a curled-up position on the floor, facing away from the robbers. Not only do robbers like it when you don't look at them, his position on his left
side enabled him to move his left hand *(his shooting hand)* to
the zipper on his fanny pack without being noticed. He care-

fully slipped the pistol out and held it under his waist—waiting his chance. As long as everything stayed relatively peaceful, he would let them take their money and get out of the bank. This is consistent with police training. The purpose of allowing robbers to exit a building before initiating contact is to avoid a shooting situation in a confined area occupied by innocent victims.

The conversation between the robber with the shotgun and the assistant bank manager was as follows:

"Open the vault, NOW!"

"The vault is on a timer."

"Don't give me that shit! I know you can open it!"

"I don't have the key to override the timer. Only the manager has that key, and he is at lunch."

"OK, we'll take one of the customers OUT," the robber yelled as he gestured to his associate.

The robber holding the revolver was near the teller cages. He lowered the gun to the thigh area of the male white-collar worker and fired one shot into his leg. Howard heard the gunfire and the scream of the wounded victim. The tellers were also screaming, but the other customers were frozen with fright. Howard believed the robber had just killed a customer to make a point, and he knew he had to act before they killed another. He thought they were likely to kill them all, once they got what they wanted out of the vault. Criminals who are desperate enough to shoot a bank customer to convince the bank employees to cooperate would be desperate enough to kill all witnesses before leaving.

Still in his "out-of-body" mode, Howard jacked a round into the chamber of his 9-mm, and rolled to his other side. His gun hand was outstretched and pointing directly at the robber holding the revolver. Without hesitation, he squeezed off two rounds to the robber's body area, and one round to his head. This was a firearm technique that the police department had adopted to take out a suspect who did not immediately fall, and to overcome those instances in which a suspect would be wearing a bulletproof vest. Howard didn't know where the first two bullets disappeared to, but he saw the third round enter the forehead area of the suspect's ski mask. His eyes opened wide, with pupils rolling up out of sight. The astonished suspect dropped like a sack of flour.

Howard rolled to his stomach and took aim at the second suspect, who had leveled the shotgun toward the floor where Howard was outstretched. Howard squeezed off two rounds as the suspect simultaneously fired both barrels at him. Two buckshot pellets tore into the top of Howard's right shoulder and exited through his armpit before he could get off that third shot to the suspect's head. The robber sank to the floor—the shotgun bouncing out of his reach. Because the shotgun had a short barrel, the eighteen buckshot pellets had spread to such a degree that only two struck the retired cop. Howard struggled to his feet to contain the fallen suspect and to protect himself against attack from the third suspect. He had suffered a serious wound to his right side; but he was left-handed and could still operate his pistol. The combined effect of the dissociative reaction and the physical shock caused him to be oblivious to the pain that should have paralyzed him. The third suspect reacted as most criminals do when the odds are even—he ran.

Forgetting his age, and the fact that he was retired, Howard was continuing to perform on "automatic pilot." He could see that the assistant manager had the presence of mind to take the shotgun further out of reach of the fallen robber. Feeling that people in the bank were safe, Howard ran out of the bank after the other suspect. What Howard was not aware of was that a teller had been able to activate a silent alarm to summon the police. As he exited the bank door, Howard was focusing on the bank robber and noticed a police car about to enter the driveway. What he did not notice, however, was a police car in the parking lot to the right of the bank doors. The officer in the parking lot was crouching behind the front fender of his car, using the car's engine for protection from any gunfire that might be directed his way. Howard had not seen him, but he heard the command, "STOP! FREEZE!"

As Howard turned to find the source of the command, the young officer saw Howard's 9-mm Colt semi-automatic pistol. He quickly squeezed off five rounds. Howard felt the hollow-point slugs enter the front of his body. He had no idea how many had struck him, but his whole upper body felt like it was on fire. He dropped his gun and fell to the pavement. Then, the pain subsided as quickly as it had started. He remained in his out-of-body mode, looking down at the horrible scene. He saw himself stretched out on the parking lot pavement. He watched as the young officer checked for a pulse at the fallen hero's carotid artery—watched as the officer checked for additional weapons—watched as the officer pulled the beat up old badge-holder wallet from the old guy's pocket, opening it to find a retirement badge and police identification card—watched as the bewildered young officer fell to his knees and sobbed uncontrollably.

Howard found that unlike the other times that he was able to return from his "out-of-body" episodes, this time he could not. He was still watching during the memorial service with full police honors that was held for him. He also watched the long funeral procession with police motorcycle escort, which resembled the escort he had participated in for his friend, Jerry. He knew his wife would understand, and that she would be comforted by the knowledge that Howard died while doing the job he so loved. He hoped others would also be comforted by that knowledge, as he had been comforted when he lost his friend—Motorcycle Officer Jerry Wyant.

Howard could now rest—thankful that he had been given the nine previous chances for survival—any one of which could have taken him before his time. Just like the cat with nine lives.

Note: See Epilogue

EPILOGUE

The fatal gun battle in a bank had been a premonition and a reoccurring nightmare for Howard, ever since the duty-related death of Jerry Wyant. Jerry's death was the turning point in Howard's life, which caused him to seriously consider the extreme danger that he faced daily. His thoughts about Jerry's motorcycle accident had generated an obsession with death and accentuated the importance of leaving the world of the living while participating in something that was meaningful to one's existence. His frequent dreams about going out in a blaze of glory had progressively become more and more vivid and life-like.

Howard would have no regrets about his life ending in a shootout with low-life, vicious bank robbers. His great dilemma is whether this gunfight was just another realistic dream—or did his premonition ultimately unfold in real life, as he suspected it someday would?

If he is really dead, then the quiet suburban life he now lives with his wife in the condominium nestled into the hillside overlooking a pristine beach on Puget Sound, and the peaceful retirement that he presently experiences, must be no more than an after-death conceptualization or vision.